INCOGNITO EXPLORERS

UNVEILING HIDDEN HORIZONS

UNRAVELLING CROATIA'S HIDDEN TREASURES

Jay Chandarana

Copyright © 2024 Jay M Chandarana

Stay connected beyond the pages – join the journey on social media

YouTube: https://www.youtube.com/@incognitodestinations
Instagram: https://www.instagram.com/incognitodestinations
Amazon Catalog: https://amazon.com/author/jaychandarana
Apple books: https://books.apple.com/us/book/revelations-in-the-soul-of-italy/id6479964311?ls=1

TABLE OF CONTENTS

Skradin-Tranquil haven, forested delights 159

Korcula: Vineyards and seascapes.................179

Reflecting on the voyage: Croatia's treasures and tales farewell..........198

Glimpsing Croatia's continued adventure: Previewing what is next....200

Journey to Croatia: Secrets unveiled; stories told

Land of a thousand stories: Croatia's opening narrative

Croatia, often hailed as the pearl of the Adriatic, presents itself as a land of boundless allure and intrigue. Nestled along the shimmering waters of the Adriatic Sea, this enchanting country boasts a captivating blend of natural beauty and cultural richness. From the charming coastal villages that dot its shores to the majestic mountains that rise in its interior, Croatia captivates the imagination with its diverse landscapes and inviting charm. Stepping foot into Croatia feels like entering a realm where ancient history and modern-day allure converge, creating an atmosphere brimming with possibilities and discovery. As visitors explore its cobblestone streets, lush vineyards, and historic landmarks, they find themselves immersed in a world where every corner tells a story, and every experience unfolds like a chapter in a grand epic.

Yet, beyond its picturesque landscapes and architectural wonders, Croatia's true essence lies in its people and their vibrant culture. Rooted in centuries-old traditions and shaped by a tumultuous history, Croatian culture is a tapestry of influences that reflect the resilience and spirit of its inhabitants. From the spirited celebrations of local festivals to the savoury delights of traditional cuisine, Croatia offers travellers a glimpse into the heart and soul of its people. With warmth and hospitality that knows no bounds, Croatians welcome visitors with open arms, eager to share their customs, stories, and joie de vivre. Thus, Croatia's opening narrative unfolds not just as a journey through geography but as an odyssey of the senses, inviting travellers to immerse themselves in the rich tapestry of its landscapes, culture, and spirit.

Ancestral echoes: Tracing Croatia's historic threads

Embarking on a journey to explore Croatia's historic threads unveils a tapestry woven with tales of resilience and cultural exchange. In Trogir, the cobbled streets wind through a UNESCO-listed Old Town, adorned with Romanesque churches and Renaissance palaces, echoing the city's past as a crossroads of civilizations and telling a story of Trogir's strategic importance as a trading port and its cultural fusion of Venetian, Hungarian, and Ottoman influences. Meanwhile, in Dubrovnik, the imposing city walls stand as guardians of a rich maritime legacy. Within the fortified enclave, visitors are transported to a bygone era of prosperity and diplomacy. Dubrovnik's cultural heritage, shaped by centuries of trade and diplomacy, offers a glimpse into a time when the city flourished as a beacon of maritime power and cultural sophistication.

As travellers traverse Croatia's coastal gems like Zadar, Hvar, and Cavtat, and inland treasures like Labin and Rovinj, they discover a land steeped in history and tradition. Zadar's ancient Roman forum bears witness to the city's enduring resilience, while Hvar's Venetian architecture and lavender fields evoke a sense of timeless beauty. In Cavtat, where the Adriatic Sea meets lush greenery, visitors are enchanted by the town's tranquillity and maritime charm. Meanwhile, Labin's medieval hilltop setting offers panoramic views of Istria's rugged landscape, a testament to the region's tumultuous past. Rovinj, with its colourful facades and bustling harbour, invites exploration of its narrow streets and hidden squares, each revealing a fragment of Croatia's storied history. Together, these destinations form a captivating narrative of Croatia's historic threads, inviting travellers to unravel the layers of its cultural heritage and embark on a journey through time.

Community mosaic: Navigating Croatia's cultural diversity

Navigating Croatia's cultural diversity is akin to embarking on a journey through a vibrant community mosaic, where each tile represents a unique aspect of the country's rich heritage. From the bustling streets of Zagreb to the tranquil villages of Istria, Croatia's landscape is adorned with a tapestry of cultures, traditions, and customs. In Zagreb, the capital city, visitors encounter a dynamic blend of Austro-Hungarian architecture, Soviet-era monuments, and contemporary art galleries, reflecting Croatia's status as a melting pot of influences from across Europe. Meanwhile, in Istria, a region known for its fertile vineyards and picturesque hilltop towns, travellers are greeted with a mix of Italian and Croatian cultures, evident in the region's cuisine, language, and way of life. As visitors traverse Croatia's diverse terrain, they become immersed in a cultural mosaic that celebrates the country's rich tapestry of identities and experiences.

Beyond the urban centres, Croatia's coastal communities offer a glimpse into the country's maritime heritage and Mediterranean charm. In Split, the ancient port city nestled along the Dalmatian Coast, visitors wander through the UNESCO-listed Diocletian's Palace, a sprawling complex that serves as a microcosm of Croatia's cultural diversity. Here, Roman ruins blend seamlessly with medieval churches and bustling markets, creating a vibrant tapestry of past and present. Further south, in Dubrovnik, the 'Pearl of the Adriatic,' travellers are transported to a world of Renaissance palaces, baroque churches, and Venetian fortifications, all set against the backdrop of the azure Adriatic Sea. Through these experiences, visitors navigate Croatia's cultural diversity, discovering the threads that bind its communities together and celebrating the mosaic of identities that define the country's collective spirit.

Pathways to wonder: Croatia's enchanting landmarks

Embarking on a journey through Croatia's enchanting destinations unveils a rich tapestry of historical and cultural landmarks. In the coastal town of Trogir, the Cathedral of St. Lawrence reigns supreme, boasting intricate Romanesque architecture and the renowned Radovan Portal. Nearby, Kamerlengo Castle stands as a silent guardian, its weathered walls echoing tales of maritime prowess and strategic defence. Within Trogir's ancient walls, St. Mark's Tower rises proudly, offering panoramic views of the town's medieval charm

Venturing inland to Labin, the Garagnin-Fanfogna Palace stands as a testament to Venetian Gothic grandeur, its graceful arcades and ornate façade reflecting centuries of aristocratic splendour. In Cavtat, the Benedictine Monastery of St. Nicholas beckons travellers to discover its tranquil cloisters and sacred relics, offering a serene retreat from the bustle of modern life. Meanwhile, in Rovinj, the Duke's Palace exudes

As the journey continues to Skradin, the ancient North Gate welcomes visitors to explore its historic streets and hidden treasures. Nearby, the Chapel of St. Sebastian offers a moment of contemplation amidst breath-taking views of the Adriatic coastline. These landmarks, scattered across Croatia's diverse landscapes, serve as beacons of wonder and discovery, inviting travellers to delve into the country's fascinating history and immerse themselves in its timeless charm.

From vineyards to seaside: Croatia's culinary voyage

Embarking on Croatia's culinary voyage unveils a gastronomic odyssey that blends the country's rich cultural heritage with its diverse landscapes. In the town of Trogir, travellers can savour the flavours of the Adriatic with fresh seafood dishes served in quaint seaside tavernas along the waterfront. Meanwhile, the bustling markets offer a bounty of local produce, from sun-ripened fruits to fragrant herbs, providing a glimpse into the vibrant culinary scene of coastal Croatia.

Further inland, the charming town of Labin beckons food enthusiasts to explore its thriving wine culture. Set amidst rolling vineyards and lush countryside, local wineries invite visitors to sample an array of indigenous varietals, from crisp white Malvazija to robust red Teran. Pairing these exquisite wines with traditional Istrian delicacies, such as truffle-infused pasta and savoury Pršut, offers a sensory journey through the heart of Croatia's culinary traditions.

Croatian compass: Guiding your journey through wonders

Navigating Croatia's wonders requires a keen understanding of its diverse landscapes, rich history, and vibrant culture. As your Croatian compass, we offer a guide to unlock the treasures awaiting discovery in this enchanting country. From the sun-kissed shores of the Adriatic to the ancient stone streets of its medieval towns, Croatia captivates with its breath-taking beauty and timeless allure. Whether you seek adventure in the rugged mountains of Dalmatia, serenity on the idyllic islands of the Kvarner Gulf, or immersion in the artistic heritage of Istria, Croatia promises an unforgettable journey filled with wonder and exploration.

Understanding Croatia's seasonal rhythms is essential for planning a rewarding visit. Spring (March to May) brings blooming wildflowers and mild temperatures, ideal for outdoor adventures and exploring historic sites without the crowds. Summer (June to August) heralds the peak tourist season, with long sunny days perfect for beach relaxation and sailing along the Adriatic coast. Autumn (September to November) offers a quieter atmosphere, with pleasant weather for hiking in national parks and indulging in harvest festivals celebrating local cuisine and wine. Winter (December to February) brings a different charm, with fewer tourists and the opportunity to experience the festive spirit of Croatian cities adorned with holiday decorations, as well as the chance to enjoy winter sports in the mountainous regions. The best time to visit Croatia depends on personal preferences, with each season offering unique experiences and attractions to suit every traveller's tastes.

When planning your visit to Croatia, consider the specific activities and experiences you desire, as well as your tolerance for crowds and weather conditions. For those seeking a lively atmosphere and vibrant beach scenes, the summer months of June to August are ideal. However, be prepared for higher prices and larger crowds at popular tourist destinations along the coast. Alternatively, if you prefer a more relaxed and authentic experience, consider visiting during the shoulder seasons of spring (March to May) or autumn (September to November). During these times, you can enjoy milder temperatures, fewer tourists, and the opportunity to immerse yourself in local culture without feeling overwhelmed by crowds.

For outdoor enthusiasts and nature lovers, spring and autumn offer excellent opportunities to explore Croatia's national parks, such as Plitvice Lakes and Krka, when the landscapes are lush and verdant. Hiking, biking, and wildlife watching are popular activities during these seasons, providing a chance to connect with Croatia's pristine natural beauty away from the summer crowds. Additionally, food and wine aficionados will delight in visiting during the autumn harvest season, when local markets brim with seasonal delights and vineyards host wine tastings showcasing Croatia's diverse wine regions.

Pack accordingly

Croatia's diverse landscapes mean that weather conditions can vary greatly depending on the region and season. Be sure to pack layers, including light clothing for summer and warmer attire for cooler months or mountainous areas. Do not forget essentials like sunscreen, a hat, sunglasses, and comfortable walking shoes for exploring cobblestone streets and natural trails.

Explore off-the-beaten-path

While popular destinations are must-sees, do not hesitate to venture off the tourist trail to discover hidden gems and lesser-known towns and villages. Explore charming coastal towns like Rovinj or inland gems like Motovun, where you can immerse yourself in local culture, sample traditional cuisine, and interact with friendly locals.

Embrace local cuisine

Croatian cuisine is a delightful fusion of Mediterranean, Central European, and Balkan influences, with fresh seafood, grilled meats, cheeses, and olive oil playing starring roles. Be sure to indulge in local specialties such as peka (slow-cooked meat or seafood with vegetables), buzara (shellfish stew), and pasticada (braised beef). Pair your meals with regional wines or rakija (fruit brandy) for an authentic culinary experience.

Respect local customs

Croatia is a country rich in tradition and heritage, and it is important to respect local customs and etiquette. When visiting churches or religious sites, dress modestly and observe quiet behaviour. When dining out, it is customary to greet your server with 'dobar dan' (good day) and to leave a small tip for good service, typically around 10% of the bill.

Stay flexible

While it is important to have a rough itinerary and plan ahead for major attractions and accommodations, allow for flexibility in your schedule to embrace spontaneous adventures and serendipitous discoveries. Croatia's beauty lies not only in its landmarks and attractions but also in the unexpected moments and experiences that await around every corner. Embrace the journey, stay open-minded, and allow Croatia to work its magic on you.

Use local transportation

Croatia offers an efficient and reliable network of buses, ferries, and trains, making it easy to explore the country without a car. Consider using public transportation or booking guided tours to navigate between cities and attractions, saving you the hassle of parking and navigation in unfamiliar areas.

Learn some basic Croatian phrases

While many Croatians speak English, making an effort to learn a few basic Croatian phrases can go a long way in enhancing your travel experience and connecting with locals. Simple greetings like 'dobar dan' (good day) and 'hvala' (thank you) are always appreciated and can help break the ice when interacting with residents.

Mind your budget

Croatia can be both affordable and luxurious, depending on your travel style and preferences. To make the most of your budget, consider dining at local restaurants away from tourist areas, where prices tend to be lower and the food is often more authentic. Additionally, look for accommodations that offer good value for money, such as guesthouses, apartments, or boutique hotels.

Stay hydrated

Croatia's Mediterranean climate means that temperatures can soar, especially during the summer months. Stay hydrated by drinking plenty of water throughout the day, especially if you'll be spending time outdoors or engaging in physical activities like hiking or sightseeing.

Respect nature

Croatia's natural beauty is one of its greatest assets, so be sure to tread lightly and leave no trace when exploring its national parks, beaches, and wilderness areas. Follow designated trails, dispose of waste responsibly, and avoid disturbing wildlife to help preserve Croatia's pristine environment for future generations to enjoy.

Be mindful of peak tourist seasons

Croatia's peak tourist season typically falls during the summer months, especially in popular coastal destinations like Dubrovnik and Hvar. Consider visiting during the shoulder seasons of spring and autumn for fewer crowds and more comfortable temperatures while still enjoying many of the country's attractions and outdoor activities.

Take advantage of free attractions

While some attractions in Croatia may require an entrance fee, there are also many free or low-cost options to explore. Stroll through historic old towns, wander along scenic coastal promenades, and soak up the atmosphere of local markets and festivals without spending a fortune.

Experience local festivals and events

Croatia hosts a variety of festivals and events throughout the year, celebrating everything from music and arts to food and culture. Check local calendars to see if any festivals coincide with your visit and immerse yourself in the vibrant energy and traditions of Croatian celebrations.

Seek authentic experiences

To truly experience the essence of Croatia, seek out authentic experiences that allow you to connect with the country's culture and heritage. Whether it is learning to make traditional dishes with a local chef, attending a folk music performance, or participating in a centuries-old festival, these immersive experiences will leave a lasting impression and enrich your travel memories

Trogir: Medieval marvel by the sea

Jay Chandarana

Unveiling Trogir's coastal timelessness and Adriatic charm

Nestled along the Dalmatian coast of Croatia, Trogir stands as a testament to centuries of maritime heritage and cultural richness. With its labyrinthine streets, well-preserved medieval architecture, and UNESCO World Heritage status, this charming town exudes an aura of coastal timelessness that captivates visitors from around the globe. From the imposing walls of the Kamerlengo Fortress to the intricate carvings of the Cathedral of St. Lawrence, every corner of Trogir tells a story of its storied past, inviting travellers to embark on a journey through history and heritage.

But Trogir's allure extends beyond its historical significance, as it boasts a stunning Adriatic backdrop that adds an extra layer of charm to its picturesque setting. The azure waters of the Adriatic Sea lap gently against the town's shores, offering breathtaking vistas and endless opportunities for relaxation and exploration. Whether strolling along the waterfront promenade, savouring fresh seafood at local tavernas, or basking in the Mediterranean sun on nearby beaches, visitors to Trogir find themselves immersed in an idyllic coastal paradise where time seems to stand still, and every moment is infused with Adriatic charm.

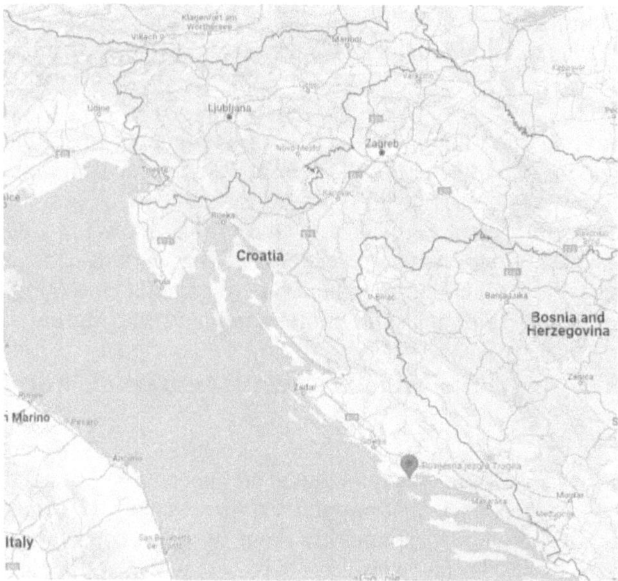

Layers of history: Trogir's eternal charm

From its ancient origins as a Greek colony to its medieval prominence as a Venetian trading hub, Trogir's rich tapestry of history is woven into every cobblestone street and centuries-old building. Wander through the alleys of the old town, and you'll encounter architectural marvels such as the Cathedral of St. Lawrence, a masterpiece of Romanesque-Gothic architecture adorned with intricate stone carvings and majestic bell towers. As you explore further, you'll stumble upon hidden gems like the Duke's Palace and the imposing Kamerlengo Fortress, each bearing witness to Trogir's storied past.

Beyond its architectural splendour, Trogir's eternal charm lies in its ability to transport visitors back in time, immersing them in the sights, sounds, and flavours of a bygone era. Lose yourself in the bustling markets, where vendors peddle local produce and artisans showcase their craftsmanship. Or pause for a moment of reflection in one of Trogir's peaceful squares, where the echoes of centuries past mingle with the gentle hum of modern life. In Trogir, history is not just a relic of the past; it is a living, breathing part of everyday existence, inviting travellers to peel back the layers and discover the timeless allure of this enchanting town.

Artistic soul: Trogir's seafaring heart and cultural harmony

At the heart of Trogir lies a deep connection to the sea, woven into the fabric of its identity as a seafaring town. From its strategic location on the Adriatic coast to its bustling harbour teeming with fishing boats and sailboats, the rhythm of life in Trogir is intertwined with the ebb and flow of the sea. Generations of seafarers have called this town home, their stories etched into the weathered facades of waterfront tavernas and maritime museums. Today, the spirit of adventure still permeates the air, beckoning travellers to set sail on the azure waters and explore the pristine islands that dot the horizon.

As visitors weave through the narrow streets of Trogir's old town, they encounter a harmonious blend of architectural styles, from Romanesque churches to Venetian palaces, each bearing witness to the town's multicultural past. Trogir's cultural heritage is celebrated through vibrant festivals and events that showcase traditional music, dance, and cuisine, inviting visitors to experience the warmth and hospitality of its people. In Trogir, the sea and culture intertwine to create a tapestry of harmony that captivates the soul and leaves a lasting impression on all who journey here.

Exploring Trogir: Unveiling architectural marvels and coastal gems

Trogir, known for its well-preserved medieval architecture and rich cultural heritage, invites travellers to step back in time and explore its narrow cobblestone streets, charming squares, and ancient landmarks. From its impressive fortress walls to its picturesque waterfront, Trogir captivates visitors with its timeless beauty and captivating atmosphere.

Cathedral of St. Lawrence

Dominating Trogir's skyline, the Cathedral of St. Lawrence is a masterpiece of Romanesque-Gothic architecture. Built over centuries, its facade is adorned with intricate sculptures, including the famous Radovan's Portal, showcasing biblical scenes and intricate details. Inside, visitors are greeted by a harmonious blend of styles, from stunning Romanesque arches to Gothic vaults. The cathedral houses an impressive collection of artworks, including Renaissance paintings and Baroque altars. Ascending the bell tower offers breath-taking views of the town and the shimmering Adriatic Sea.

St. Mark's tower

Guarding the entrance to Trogir's old town, St. Mark's Tower is a formidable structure dating back to the 15th century. Rising majestically above the city gates, it served as a vital defensive outpost against invaders. The tower's robust stone walls and battlements reflect the town's turbulent history and enduring resilience. Today, it stands as a symbol of Trogir's medieval heritage, inviting visitors to step back in time and envision the town's past defences.

The town loggia

Located in the heart of Trogir's old town square, the town loggia is a symbol of civic pride and communal gathering. Dating back to the Venetian era, this elegant Renaissance structure served as a meeting place for local dignitaries and merchants. Its graceful arches and open-air design invite visitors to linger, soaking in the ambiance of the historic square and admiring the surrounding architectural splendour.

Kamerlengo castle

Built by the Venetians in the 15th century as a defensive fortress, Kamerlengo castle stands proudly on the waterfront, its sturdy stone walls a testament to Trogir's maritime heritage. The castle's strategic location offers commanding views of the Adriatic coast and nearby islands. Visitors can explore its well-preserved ramparts, climb the towers for panoramic vistas, and wander through the courtyard, imagining the castle's storied past as a bastion of defence and power.

Trogir town museum

Housed within the historic Garagnin-Fanfogna palace, the Trogir town museum offers a fascinating journey through the town's history and culture. Its exhibits showcase archaeological finds, historical artifacts, and artworks spanning centuries. Visitors can delve into Trogir's maritime heritage, medieval craftsmanship, and rich artistic traditions.

Benedictine monastery of St. Nicholas

Situated on the island of Čiovo, just a short distance from Trogir, the Benedictine monastery of St. Nicholas is a tranquil haven of spirituality and beauty. Dating back to the 11th century, the monastery's Romanesque architecture and serene cloister invite contemplation and reflection. Visitors can explore its peaceful courtyard, admire its religious artworks, and learn about its centuries-old legacy.

Chapel of Blessed John of Trogir

Nestled within the walls of Kamerlengo Castle, the Chapel of Blessed John of Trogir is a hidden gem of spiritual significance. Dedicated to Blessed John, a medieval Dominican friar revered for his piety and miracles, the chapel offers a serene space for prayer and meditation. It is simple yet elegant interior, adorned with sacred art and candlelight, evokes a sense of reverence and devotion.

The Duke's palace (Cipiko palace)

Nestled within Trogir's streets, the Duke's palace is a striking example of Renaissance architecture. Built by the noble Cipiko family in the 15th century, the palace exudes opulence with its graceful arcades, ornate façade, and elegant courtyard. Once a seat of power and prestige, it now houses cultural exhibitions and events, offering visitors a glimpse into Trogir's aristocratic past and artistic legacy.

The Cipiko garden

Tucked away behind the Duke's palace, the Cipiko garden is a hidden oasis of peace and beauty in the heart of Trogir. This verdant sanctuary features lush greenery, fragrant flowers, and tranquil water features, providing a serene escape from the bustling streets. Visitors can stroll along winding pathways, relax on shaded benches, and admire the timeless elegance of this historic garden.

Savouring Adriatic bounty: Trogir's coastal culinary delights

Embark on a culinary journey through the streets of Trogir, where the vibrant colours and tantalizing aromas of Mediterranean cuisine beckon travellers to indulge in a feast for the senses. From quaint seaside tavernas to bustling market stalls, Trogir's culinary scene reflects the town's rich cultural heritage and coastal bounty. Prepare to tantalize your taste buds with an array of fresh seafood, locally sourced ingredients, and traditional recipes passed down through generations.

Fresh seafood

Trogir's coastal location means that fresh seafood is a staple in many local dishes. Grilled fish, seafood risotto, and black cuttlefish risotto are just a few examples of the seafood dishes you can try in Trogir's restaurants. The fish is often caught daily and served with locally-grown vegetables, creating a delicious and healthy meal.

Fritule

These small, fried dough balls are a popular dessert in Trogir. They are often served with ice cream or a dusting of powdered sugar. They are made with flour, eggs, sugar, and a variety of flavourings, such as rum, citrus zest, or raisins. They are a delicious and indulgent way to end a meal in Trogir.

Rakija

This strong, clear brandy is a popular drink in Croatia and is often made from grapes, plums, or other fruits. It is often served as a digestif after a meal and is a great way to warm up on a cool evening. Rakija is a traditional drink in Croatia and is a must-try in Trogir.

Soparnik

This traditional Dalmatian dish is a savoury pie made with chard, onions, garlic, and olive oil. The filling is wrapped in a thin layer of dough and baked until crispy. Soparnik is a popular dish in Dalmatia and is often served as a side dish or a light lunch. It is a vegetarian dish that is full of flavour and is a must-try in Trogir.

Pasticada

This traditional Dalmatian stew is made with beef, wine, and a variety of herbs and spices. It is slow-cooked to perfection and served with gnocchi or pasta. The beef is marinated in garlic, onions, and herbs before being cooked with red wine, tomatoes, and prunes. The result is a rich and flavourful stew that is a must-try in Trogir. It is often served with a side of polenta or mashed potatoes.

Buzara

This seafood dish is made with clams, mussels, shrimp, and squid, cooked in a white wine and garlic sauce. It is a popular dish in Dalmatia and is often served with pasta or bread. Buzara is a light and flavourful dish that is perfect for seafood lovers. The seafood is cooked in a white wine and garlic sauce, which gives it a light and aromatic flavour.

Kobasica

This traditional Dalmatian sausage is made with pork, garlic, and paprika. It is often served as an appetizer or a side dish and is a staple in Dalmatian cuisine. Kobasica is a savoury and spicy dish that is a must-try in Trogir. The sausage is typically served cold and is often accompanied by a side of pickled vegetables or a glass of local beer.

Marasca

This traditional Dalmatian liqueur is made with marasca cherries, which are grown in the region. It is often served as a digestif after a meal and is a popular drink in Dalmatia. Marasca is a sweet and fruity liqueur that is a must-try in Trogir. The liqueur is typically served in small glasses and is often accompanied by a side of almonds or a piece of chocolate.

Peka

This traditional Dalmatian dish is a slow-cooked stew made with meat, potatoes, and vegetables, cooked under a bell-shaped lid. The dish is typically made with lamb, but beef or chicken can also be used. Peka is a hearty and flavourful dish that is a must-try in Trogir. It is often served with a side of polenta or bread.

Prosciutto

This traditional Dalmatian ham is made with pork that is been cured with salt and air-dried. It is often served as an appetizer or a side dish and is a staple in Dalmatian cuisine. Prosciutto is a savoury and salty dish that is a must-try in Trogir. It is often served with a side of fresh bread or crackers and is a popular snack in Croatia.

Prsut

This dry-cured ham is a staple in Croatian cuisine and is often served as an appetizer. Trogir's prsut is known for its high quality and is often paired with local cheeses and olives. It is made from the hind legs of pigs and is cured with sea salt and smoke. Pršut is often served with a side of fresh bread or crackers and is a popular snack in Croatia.

In Trogir, culinary delights are not just meals but experiences that celebrate the region's rich culinary heritage and vibrant flavours. From the savoury depths of black risotto to the rustic charm of peka, each dish tells a story of tradition, passion, and the bountiful treasures of the Adriatic coast. As you savour the flavours of Trogir, you'll discover a culinary paradise that invites you to indulge in the simple pleasures of good food and great company.

Uncovering coastal treasures: Trogir's hidden gems await

Beyond the bustling streets and popular attractions of Trogir lies a world of hidden gems, each waiting to be uncovered by those with a keen eye for the extraordinary. From ancient portals to secluded chapels, these hidden treasures offer a glimpse into the town's past and present, inviting visitors to delve deeper into its history and charm.

The Cat and Mouse tower

This unique tower is located on the western side of Trogir's Old Town and is a great place to explore if you are interested in history and architecture. The Cat and Mouse Tower is a part of the ancient city walls that once protected Trogir from invaders. The tower is named after the cat and mouse carvings on the tower's exterior, which are said to represent the struggle between good and evil.

St. Barbara's cathedral

This stunning cathedral is located in the heart of Trogir's Old Town and is one of the most impressive examples of Romanesque-Gothic architecture in the area. The St. Barbara's Cathedral was built in the 13th century and is home to a beautiful bell tower and a stunning interior. The cathedral is named after St. Barbara, who is the patron saint of Trogir.

Convent of St. Nicholas

This beautiful convent is located on the eastern side of Trogir's Old Town. The Convent of St. Nicholas was founded in the 16th century and is home to a beautiful cloister and a stunning Baroque church. The convent is open to the public for guided tours and is a must-see for anyone interested in the history of Trogir and the surrounding area.

Church of St. Peter

The Church of St. Peter was built in the 12th century and is home to a stunning collection of Romanesque art and architecture. The church is open to the public for guided tours and is a must-see for anyone interested in the history of Trogir and the surrounding area.

Marmont's glory monument

Nestled in the heart of Trogir's historic centre, the Marmont's Glory Monument stands as a tribute to the town's rich history and enduring resilience. Erected in the early 19th century under the reign of Napoleon's Marshal Marmont, the monument showcases intricate details and elegant design, reflecting the town's architectural splendour. Visitors can admire its neoclassical facade and symbolic significance, evoking a sense of pride and reverence for Trogir's past.

St. Mark's tower

Rising majestically above the rooftops of Trogir, the St. Mark's Tower offers panoramic views of the town's picturesque landscape and surrounding Adriatic Sea. Built during the Venetian era, this imposing structure served as a defensive fortification, guarding the town against potential threats from the sea. Today, visitors can ascend the tower's narrow staircase to reach its rooftop terrace, where they can marvel at the breath-taking vistas and immerse themselves in Trogir's timeless beauty.

St. John's tower

Tucked away in a quiet corner of Trogir's old town, the St. John's Tower exudes an aura of mystery and intrigue. Dating back to the medieval period, this ancient tower once formed part of the town's formidable defensive walls, providing shelter and protection to its inhabitants. Today, the tower stands as a silent sentinel, offering glimpses into Trogir's storied past and inviting visitors to step back in time as they explore its weathered walls and hidden chambers.

Monastery of St. Dominic

This stunning monastery is located on the eastern side of Trogir's Old Town. The monastery is open to the public and offers guided tours that provide insight into the history and architecture of the building. The Monastery of St. Dominic was founded in the 13th century and is home to a beautiful Gothic cloister and a stunning Baroque church. The monastery also houses a museum that showcases the history of Trogir and the surrounding area.

Trogir is a charming coastal town in Croatia that is known for its stunning architecture and rich history. However, there are also several hidden gems that are worth exploring and there is something for every traveller to enjoy in Trogir. Whether you are interested in history, architecture, or just exploring a new place, these hidden gems are sure to provide a memorable experience.

Seaside escapades: Trogir's outdoor thrills and spectacular views

Trogir's stunning coastline and picturesque countryside offer a wealth of opportunities for outdoor activities. From water sports such as sailing, swimming, and snorkelling to land-based adventures such as hiking, biking, and rock climbing, there is no shortage of ways to explore the region's natural beauty. Whether you are looking for a thrilling adventure or a peaceful retreat in nature, Trogir's outdoor activities are sure to leave you with unforgettable memories.

Hiking in Kozjak mountain

Lace up your boots and explore the pristine wilderness of Kozjak Mountain, located just inland from Trogir. Trek along scenic trails that wind through lush forests and rugged terrain, offering panoramic views of the Adriatic coastline and surrounding islands. Whether you are a seasoned hiker or a novice explorer, Kozjak Mountain promises an unforgettable outdoor adventure.

Snorkelling in Blue Lagoon

Discover the vibrant underwater world of the Blue Lagoon, a crystal-clear bay near Trogir renowned for its azure waters and colourful marine life. Grab your snorkel gear and immerse yourself in the tranquil sea, where you'll encounter a kaleidoscope of fish, sea turtles, and fascinating coral formations. With its calm waters and shallow depths, the Blue Lagoon is an ideal spot for snorkelers of all skill levels to experience the beauty of Croatia's Adriatic coast.

Sailing around the islands

Set sail on a nautical adventure around the picturesque islands that dot the waters near Trogir. Rent a sailboat or join a guided tour to explore hidden coves, secluded beaches, and charming fishing villages tucked away along the coastline. Feel the wind in your hair as you glide across the Adriatic Sea.

Rock climbing in Marjan hill

Marjan Hill, located near Split and easily accessible from Trogir, offers a thrilling rock-climbing experience amidst stunning coastal scenery. Climbers of all skill levels

can find routes suited to their abilities, from beginner-friendly to more challenging ascents. As you scale the rugged cliffs of Marjan, you'll be rewarded with panoramic views of the Adriatic Sea and nearby island.

Jet skiing in the Adriatic

Feel the wind in your hair and the spray of the sea as you zip across the azure waters of the Adriatic Sea on a jet ski adventure. With Trogir as your starting point, you can rent a jet ski and explore the coastline at your own pace, discovering hidden coves, secluded beaches, and charming seaside villages along the way. Whether you are a thrill-seeker looking for high-speed excitement or simply craving a fun-filled day on the water, jet skiing in the Adriatic promises an exhilarating experience.

Parasailing above Čiovo island

Take your Trogir adventure to new heights with a parasailing excursion above the scenic waters surrounding Čiovo Island. As you ascend into the sky beneath a colourful parachute, you'll enjoy breath-taking views of Trogir's historic old town, shimmering coastline, and lush green landscapes stretching to the horizon. Whether you are a first-time flyer or a seasoned thrill-seeker, parasailing offers an unforgettable perspective on the beauty of the Dalmatian coast.

Cycling through vineyards and olive groves

Discover the scenic beauty and cultural heritage of Trogir's countryside on a cycling tour through lush vineyards and ancient olive groves. Pedal along quiet country roads and picturesque trails, stopping to sample local wines, olive oils, and traditional Croatian cuisine at family-owned farms and wineries along the way.

Birdwatching in Pantan wetland

Immerse yourself in the serene beauty of Pantan Wetland, a protected nature reserve located just outside of Trogir, renowned for its rich biodiversity and diverse bird species. As you wander along wooden boardwalks and nature trails, you'll have the opportunity to observe a variety of birdlife, including herons, egrets, and migratory birds, in their natural habitat.

Kayaking in Trogir Bay

Explore the scenic beauty of Trogir Bay from a unique perspective on a kayaking adventure. Paddle along the tranquil waters, passing by ancient Venetian walls, charming waterfront villas, and picturesque islands. With Trogir's stunning coastline as your backdrop, kayaking offers a peaceful and immersive way to discover hidden coves, secluded beaches, and vibrant marine life beneath the crystal-clear waters.

Yachting excursions to Vis Island

Set sail on a yachting excursion to Vis Island, one of the most remote and unspoiled islands in the Adriatic Sea. Cruise along the sparkling waters aboard a luxurious yacht, stopping to swim in secluded bays, snorkel in crystal-clear lagoons, and explore hidden beaches accessible only by boat. With its pristine landscapes, charming fishing villages, and rich history, Vis Island offers a tranquil and enchanting escape from the hustle and bustle of mainland Croatia.

Zip-lining in Omis canyon

Embark on an adrenaline-pumping zip-lining adventure in the rugged landscapes of Omiš Canyon, located just a short drive from Trogir. Soar high above the canyon floor on a series of exhilarating zip-line cables, enjoying breath-taking views of the Cetina River, lush forests, and towering cliffs below. With professional guides and state-of-the-art safety equipment, zip-lining in Omiš Canyon promises an unforgettable outdoor experience for thrill-seekers and nature lovers alike.

Sunset sailing cruise along Trogir coast

Unwind and relax on a sunset sailing cruise along the picturesque coast of Trogir, where you can enjoy breath-taking views of the Adriatic Sea as the sun dips below the horizon. Set sail aboard a traditional wooden boat or modern catamaran, sipping cocktails and enjoying delicious Croatian cuisine as you glide past ancient landmarks, secluded coves, and idyllic islands bathed in the golden glow of the setting sun.

In Trogir, the great outdoors beckon with endless possibilities for adventure and relaxation. Whether you are scaling mountain peaks, exploring underwater realms, or sailing into the sunset, the town's natural beauty provides the perfect backdrop for unforgettable outdoor experiences. So, pack your sense of adventure and get ready to explore the wonders of Trogir's outdoor playground.

Celebrating coastal heritage: Trogir's vibrant festivals

Trogir's cultural calendar is filled with a variety of events that cater to different interests and tastes. Whether you are a history buff, a foodie, an art lover, or a music enthusiast, there is something for everyone in Trogir's vibrant cultural scene. These festivals and traditions offer a unique and authentic experience that goes beyond the town's picturesque streets and historic landmarks.

Kucanje

Kućanje is a cherished New Year's tradition in Trogir where groups of friends and family members embark on a jovial journey through the town's streets. Armed with musical instruments and traditional songs, they knock on doors, spreading blessings and good wishes for the year ahead. This heart-warming custom foster camaraderie and unity among neighbours, symbolizing the spirit of togetherness that defines Trogir's community.

Gospa od Prizidnice

Gospa od Prizidnice pays homage to its maritime heritage and religious devotion through the celebration of Gospa od Prizidnice, the feast day of Our Lady of Prizidnica. The day begins with a solemn procession, where locals and pilgrims gather to honour the town's patron saint. Following the religious ceremonies, the atmosphere transforms into one of festivity, with music, dance, and delectable local cuisine adding to the joyful ambiance.

Ribarska Fešta

Ribarska Fešta celebrates Trogir's deep connection to the sea and its proud fishing heritage. Held annually, this lively festival brings together locals and visitors alike to indulge in a feast of freshly caught seafood, prepared according to age-old recipes. Boat parades, fishing competitions, and maritime-themed entertainment add to the maritime festivities, offering a glimpse into the vibrant culture of Trogir's waterfront.

Trogirsko Ljeto

Trogirsko Ljeto bathes the town in a vibrant tapestry of cultural events throughout the summer months. From enchanting concerts in historic squares to captivating theatre performances in ancient palaces, the festival showcases the rich artistic heritage of Trogir. Visitors are invited to immerse themselves in the creative energy of the town, savouring culinary delights, admiring local artwork, and experiencing the warmth of Trogir's hospitality.

Trogirski Karneval

Trogirski Karneval transforms the streets of Trogir into a colourful spectacle of costumes, music, and dance during the carnival season. Locals and visitors alike don masks and elaborate outfits, joining in lively parades and street parties that celebrate joy, creativity, and community spirit.

Sveti Ivan

Sveti Ivan is celebrated in honour of St. John the Baptist, the patron saint of Trogir. The day begins with religious services at the town's churches, followed by lively festivities that include music, dancing, and traditional games. One of the highlights of the celebration is the lighting of bonfires along the coast, a symbolic ritual that dates back to ancient times and represents the triumph of light over darkness.

Fešta Karmela

Fešta Karmela honours St. Carmel, the patron saint of Trogir, on July 16th with a blend of religious solemnity and festive revelry. The day begins with solemn religious ceremonies, including a procession through the town's historic streets adorned with colourful banners and floral displays. As evening falls, the atmosphere transforms into one of joyous celebration, with traditional music, dance performances, and cultural exhibitions adding to the festivities.

Festival klapa

Trogir hosts an annual Klapa Music Festival celebrating the traditional acapella singing style known as klapa. Groups from across Croatia gather to perform soulful melodies and harmonies in Trogir's historic squares and waterfront promenades. The festival highlights the importance of klapa music in Croatian culture, fostering appreciation for this unique art form while showcasing the talents of local musicians and singers.

Trogirski Filmski Festival

The Trogir Film Festival is an annual event that celebrates the art of cinema in the historic setting of Trogir. Held over several days, the festival showcases a diverse selection of national and international films, ranging from feature-length dramas to documentaries and short films. Screenings take place in iconic venues throughout the town, offering attendees the opportunity to enjoy cinematic masterpieces against the backdrop of Trogir's stunning architecture and scenic beauty.

Trogirski Festival Brodova

The Trogir Boat Festival is an annual celebration of the town's maritime heritage and seafaring traditions. Held in the summer months, the festival features a colourful procession of boats decorated with flags and banners, parading through the waters of Trogir's harbour. Spectators gather along the waterfront to admire the vessels and cheer on the sailors, creating a festive atmosphere filled with music, laughter, and camaraderie.

In Trogir, traditions are more than just events; they are living expressions of the town's cultural identity and collective memory. Whether it is the joyful melodies of Kucanje, the solemn processions of Gospa od Prizidnice, or the artistic flair of Trogirsko Ljeto, each tradition adds a unique dimension to the vibrant tapestry of Trogir's cultural landscape. Visitors are invited to immerse themselves in these timeless customs, forging connections with the past while celebrating the present spirit of Trogir.

Unlocking Trogir's secrets: Essential travel tips revealed

Planning a trip to Trogir? Get ready to experience the magic of this charming Croatian town nestled along the Dalmatian coast. To make the most of your visit, here are some invaluable travel tips that will ensure a smooth and unforgettable journey.

Currency and payment methods

In Trogir, the official currency is the Croatian Kuna (HRK). While many establishments, especially in tourist areas, accept credit and debit cards, it is wise to carry some cash for smaller purchases and transactions, as not all businesses may have card facilities. ATMs are readily available throughout Trogir, allowing you to withdraw cash conveniently in local currency.

Language and communication

Croatian is the official language of Croatia, including Trogir, but English is widely spoken in tourist areas. Basic English proficiency among locals makes communication relatively easy for international visitors. However, learning a few basic Croatian phrases, such as greetings and simple questions, can enhance your interactions and show appreciation for the local culture. Locals often appreciate the effort to speak their language, no matter how basic your skills may be.

Local transportation

Trogir offers various transportation options for getting around the town and exploring nearby attractions. Within Trogir, walking is a popular and convenient way to navigate its narrow cobblestone streets and historic landmarks. Bicycle rentals are also available for those who prefer two-wheeled exploration, providing a leisurely means to discover the town and its scenic coastline. Additionally, taxis, buses, and water taxis offer convenient transportation to neighbouring areas and islands, allowing you to explore further afield.

Weather and packing essentials

Trogir enjoys a Mediterranean climate, characterized by hot, dry summers and mild winters. When visiting during the summer months, lightweight and breathable clothing is essential to stay comfortable in the warm temperatures. Do not forget to pack sunscreen, sunglasses, and a wide-brimmed hat to protect yourself from the sun's intense rays, especially if you plan to spend time outdoors.

Respect local customs and culture

Trogir boasts a rich cultural heritage, and it is important for visitors to respect local customs and traditions. When visiting religious sites, such as churches and monasteries, dress modestly and refrain from wearing revealing clothing out of respect for the sacredness of these places. Additionally, always ask for permission before taking photos of locals, as some may prefer not to be photographed.

Safety and emergency contacts

Trogir is generally a safe destination for travellers, but it is always important to take precautions to ensure your safety. Be vigilant of your surroundings, especially in crowded tourist areas, and keep your belongings secure to avoid pickpocketing and theft. In case of emergency, dial 112 for assistance, which is the universal emergency number in Croatia. Additionally, familiarize yourself with the location of the nearest medical facilities and pharmacies, should you require medical assistance during your stay.

Environmental conservation and responsible tourism

As a responsible traveller, it is important to minimize your environmental impact and support sustainable practices during your visit to Trogir. Respect the natural surroundings by avoiding littering and disposing of waste properly. Consider participating in eco-friendly activities, such as beach clean-ups and nature conservation projects, to contribute positively to the local community and environment.

Shopping and souvenirs

Take home a piece of Trogir's charm by exploring its local shops and markets for unique souvenirs and gifts. Wander through the narrow streets of the old town to discover boutiques selling handmade crafts, artwork, and traditional Croatian products such as lace, olive oil, and lavender products. Do not forget to haggle politely at local markets for the best deals on handmade goods and locally sourced produce.

Health and travel insurance

Prioritize your health and well-being during your trip to Trogir by ensuring you have adequate travel insurance coverage. While Croatia has a reliable healthcare system, it is recommended to have comprehensive travel insurance that covers medical

emergencies, trip cancellations, and personal liability. Carry a copy of your insurance policy and emergency contact information with you at all times for peace of mind during your travels.

Internet and connectivity

Stay connected with family and friends back home by taking advantage of Trogir's internet and connectivity options. Many accommodations, cafes, and restaurants offer free Wi-Fi for guests, allowing you to stay connected while exploring the town. If you require constant internet access during your stay, consider purchasing a local SIM card with data plans from one of Croatia's major mobile network providers for reliable internet connectivity on the go.

With these travel tips in mind, you are well-equipped to embark on an unforgettable journey to Trogir. Whether you are strolling through its cobblestone streets, lounging on its sun-kissed beaches, or savouring its delicious cuisine, Trogir promises a magical experience that will leave you longing to return again and again. Safe travels and enjoy your adventure in this enchanting Croatian gem!

Until next time: Trogir's coastal allure lingers

In Trogir, every cobblestone street, every historic building, and every shimmering wave holds a story waiting to be discovered. As you carry the essence of Trogir with you, may the memories of its cultural riches, culinary delights, and natural wonders continue to inspire and captivate your heart, reminding you of the beauty and magic found in this hidden gem along Croatia's Dalmatian coast. Whether it is the echoes of ancient civilizations, the taste of fresh seafood, or the sight of a radiant sunset over the Adriatic Sea, Trogir's closing thoughts are a symphony of experiences that resonate with the soul and beckon you to return to its embrace.

As you conclude your exploration of Trogir, a town brimming with history, culture, and natural beauty, take a moment to reflect on the memories you've created and the experiences you've savoured. Trogir's timeless charm, from its ancient streets to its picturesque waterfront, leaves an indelible mark on visitors, inviting them to immerse themselves in its rich tapestry of traditions and heritage. The warmth of the locals, the flavours of its culinary delights, and the serenity of its coastal landscapes combine to

create a lasting impression that lingers long after you've bid farewell to this enchanting coastal gem.

Dubrovnik: Harbour of legends, coastal sanctuary

Embark on a journey: Dubrovnik's coastal enchantment

Embark on an enchanting journey through the coastal gem of Dubrovnik, where history, culture, and natural beauty intertwine to create an unforgettable experience. Nestled along the azure waters of the Adriatic Sea, Dubrovnik captivates visitors with its medieval charm and stunning coastal vistas. As you wander through the ancient streets of the Old Town, you'll be transported back in time, surrounded by centuries-old architecture, charming alleyways, and hidden courtyards waiting to be discovered.

But Dubrovnik's allure extends beyond its historical significance, offering a myriad of activities to indulge in its coastal enchantment. From leisurely walks along the iconic city walls, offering panoramic views of the shimmering sea and terracotta rooftops, to basking in the sun on the picturesque Banje Beach, every moment in Dubrovnik is infused with the magic of the Mediterranean. Whether you are exploring the historic landmarks, savouring local delicacies at seaside cafes, or simply soaking in the coastal ambiance, Dubrovnik invites you to embark on a journey of discovery unlike any other.

Dubrovnik's ancient splendour: Stories etched in stone

Step back in time and immerse yourself in the ancient splendour of Dubrovnik, a city where stories are etched in stone and every corner whispers tales of bygone eras. As you traverse the cobblestone streets of the Old Town, you'll be transported to a time of medieval grandeur, where towering city walls and imposing fortresses stand as guardians of a rich and storied past. From the majestic architecture of the Rector's Palace to the intricate carvings of the Franciscan Monastery, Dubrovnik's ancient landmarks offer a glimpse into the city's illustrious history.

But beyond its architectural marvels, Dubrovnik's ancient splendour is also reflected in its vibrant cultural scene and time-honoured traditions. Discover the echoes of the past in the vibrant colours of the local markets, where artisans sell handcrafted goods and fresh produce harvested from the surrounding countryside. Immerse yourself in the rhythms of traditional folk music and dance, or sample the flavours of Dubrovnik's culinary heritage at charming tavernas tucked away in hidden alleys. In Dubrovnik, the past comes alive, inviting visitors to become part of its timeless narrative and experience the magic of ancient splendour first-hand.

Sailing through time: Dubrovnik's cultural odyssey

Discover the treasures of the Adriatic as you journey through Dubrovnik, a city adorned with landmarks that unveil the rich tapestry of its history and culture. From the imposing walls of the Dubrovnik Old Town to the iconic red-roofed houses that line its streets, every corner of this coastal gem holds a story waiting to be told. Wander through the labyrinthine alleys of the Old Town and marvel at architectural wonders like the Sponza Palace and the Onofrio Fountain, each a testament to Dubrovnik's medieval splendour.

But Dubrovnik's allure goes beyond its architectural beauty, as its landmarks also serve as guardians of the city's cultural heritage. Explore the centuries-old traditions of Dubrovnik at the bustling Stradun, where local artisans showcase their crafts and street performers entertain passers-by with traditional music and dance. Ascend to the summit of Mount Srd for panoramic views of the city and the shimmering Adriatic Sea, or visit the historic Dubrovnik Cathedral to admire its stunning architecture and exquisite artwork. In Dubrovnik, the treasures of the Adriatic await, ready to be unveiled by those who dare to explore its storied streets and landmarks.

Treasures of the Adriatic: Dubrovnik's landmarks unveiled

Dubrovnik, a stunning coastal city in Croatia, is known for its rich history, architectural marvels, and breath-taking natural beauty. With its well-preserved Old Town, a UNESCO World Heritage site, and a variety of landmarks and points of interest, Dubrovnik offers a captivating experience for travellers. From the ancient city walls to the pristine beaches of the Elaphite Islands, Dubrovnik's attractions are a testament to its rich cultural heritage and natural beauty. Old Town Walls (Gradske zidine) stretches over 1,940 meters in length and reaches heights of up to 25 meters and offer panoramic views of the city and the Adriatic Sea.

Lovrijenac fortress

Perched on a cliff overlooking the Adriatic Sea, Lovrijenac Fortress is a formidable defensive structure that has guarded the city of Dubrovnik for centuries. Built in the 11th century, the fortress boasts impressive walls, towers, and bastions, and offers breath-taking views of Dubrovnik's Old Town and the surrounding coastline. Today, Lovrijenac Fortress serves as a venue for cultural events, including the Dubrovnik Summer Festival, and is a must-visit for history enthusiasts and photographers alike.

Sponza palace

Sponza Palace is a Renaissance-era palace located in Dubrovnik's Old Town, renowned for its elegant architecture and historical significance. Built in the 16th century, the palace served as a customs house, mint, and treasury during the time of the Republic of Ragusa. Today, Sponza Palace houses the Dubrovnik State Archives, where visitors can explore a wealth of historical documents, manuscripts, and artifacts that offer insights into Dubrovnik's past and cultural heritage.

Stradun

Stradun, also known as Placa, is the main thoroughfare and heart of Dubrovnik's Old Town. This limestone-paved street stretches from the Pile Gate to the Ploče Gate, lined with elegant Baroque buildings, charming cafes, and souvenir shops. As you stroll along Stradun, you'll be immersed in the vibrant atmosphere of Dubrovnik, with street performers, bustling crowds, and the sound of church bells echoing in the air. It is the perfect place to experience the timeless charm and lively energy of the city.

Dubrovnik city walls

In addition to the Old Town Walls, Dubrovnik is also famous for its City Walls, which extend beyond the historic centre and offer stunning views of the city and the Adriatic Sea. Dating back to the 9th century, these walls were fortified and expanded over the centuries to protect Dubrovnik from invasions. Visitors can walk along the walls and admire the watchtowers, fortresses, and defensive towers that dot the landscape, gaining a deeper appreciation for Dubrovnik's architectural and military history.

Franciscan monastery and pharmacy

The Franciscan Monastery is one of Dubrovnik's most important religious and cultural landmarks, dating back to the 14th century. Admire the monastery's elegant cloisters, Gothic architecture, and stunning works of art, including a masterpiece by the Renaissance painter Titian. Do not miss the chance to visit the monastery's ancient pharmacy, which has been in operation since the 14th century and is one of the oldest continuously operating pharmacies in Europe.

Dubrovnik cathedral

Dominating the skyline of Dubrovnik's Old Town is the magnificent Dubrovnik Cathedral, dedicated to the Assumption of the Virgin Mary. Built in the 17th century on the site of a former Romanesque cathedral, the cathedral showcases exquisite Baroque architecture and a stunning interior adorned with marble altars, intricate sculptures, and magnificent artwork. Visitors can admire the cathedral's ornate facade, bell tower, and treasury, which houses a collection of religious relics and artifacts.

St. Blaise church

St. Blaise Church is a Baroque-style church dedicated to the patron saint of Dubrovnik, St. Blaise. Located in the heart of the Old Town, the church is known for its distinctive dome and elegant facade adorned with statues of saints. Inside, visitors can admire ornate altars, intricate carvings, and beautiful frescoes depicting scenes from the life of St. Blaise. The church is a symbol of Dubrovnik's religious devotion and cultural identity.

Dubrovnik cable car

For panoramic views of Dubrovnik and the surrounding Adriatic Sea, take a ride on the Dubrovnik Cable Car. The cable car ascends to the summit of Mount Srđ, offering breath-taking vistas of the Old Town, Lokrum Island, and the Dalmatian coastline. At the top, visitors can enjoy refreshments at the panoramic restaurant, explore the Fort Imperial, and learn about Dubrovnik's history at the Museum of the Homeland War.

Rector's palace

Rector's Palace is a historic landmark that served as the seat of the Rector of the Republic of Ragusa, the governing authority of Dubrovnik, during the medieval period. Built in the Gothic-Renaissance style in the 15th century, the palace features a striking facade adorned with sculptures, columns, and coats of arms. Today, Rector's Palace houses the Museum of Dubrovnik, where visitors can explore its elegant chambers, impressive staircases, and exhibits showcasing the city's history, culture, and traditions.

Dubrovnik synagogue

Dubrovnik Synagogue is one of the oldest Sephardic synagogues in Europe and a testament to the city's multicultural heritage. Built in the 15th century, the synagogue features a blend of Gothic and Renaissance architecture, with an interior adorned with richly decorated ceilings and Hebrew inscriptions. Visitors can learn about Dubrovnik's Jewish community and its history through exhibits and artifacts displayed in the adjacent Jewish Museum.

Onofrio's fountain

Located near the Pile Gate in Dubrovnik's Old Town, Onofrio's Fountain is a striking example of Renaissance architecture and engineering. Built in the 15th century by the Italian architect Onofrio della Cava, the fountain once supplied fresh water to the city via a sophisticated aqueduct system. Today, Onofrio's Fountain serves as a gathering place for locals and visitors alike, who come to admire its elegant design and enjoy a refreshing drink from its cool waters.

Dubrovnik's landmarks and points of interest are a testament to the city's rich cultural heritage and natural beauty, offering visitors a captivating experience that combines history, architecture, and breath-taking views. From the ancient city walls to the pristine beaches of the Elaphite Islands, Dubrovnik's attractions are a must-visit for any traveller seeking to explore the beauty and charm of Croatia's Dalmatian coast.

Dubrovnik's coastal palette: A culinary adventure

Dubrovnik's culinary scene is a tantalizing fusion of fresh seafood, savoury meats, and vibrant Mediterranean flavours, drawing inspiration from centuries-old recipes passed down through generations. From quaint family-owned tavernas to upscale dining establishments, the city offers an array of culinary delights that promise to delight even the most discerning food enthusiasts.

Black risotto

Black risotto is a beloved dish in Dubrovnik, renowned for its rich flavours and striking appearance. Made with Arborio rice, squid ink, garlic, onions, white wine, and seafood broth, this dish boasts a deep, savoury taste reminiscent of the Adriatic Sea. Tender pieces of squid add a delightful texture, while the aromatic blend of herbs and spices enhances the overall experience. Served hot and garnished with fresh parsley or grated Parmesan cheese, black risotto is a must-try for seafood lovers visiting Dubrovnik.

Dalmatian peka

Dalmatian peka is a traditional Croatian dish that epitomizes the simplicity and rustic charm of Mediterranean cuisine. Meat, usually lamb or veal, and vegetables such as potatoes, carrots, and onions, are seasoned with olive oil, garlic, rosemary, and other herbs and spices. The ingredients are then placed in a cast-iron bell or 'peka' and slow-roasted over hot coals, allowing the flavours to meld together and the meat to become tender and succulent.

Brodetto Dubrovnik style

Brodetto is a traditional Dalmatian seafood stew, but Dubrovnik's version adds its own unique flair. The stew is prepared with a variety of locally caught seafood, such as fish, shrimp, and shellfish, simmered in a savoury tomato-based broth flavoured with garlic, onions, and aromatic herbs. What sets Dubrovnik's brodetto apart is the addition of local Dubrovnik liqueur, giving the dish a subtle sweetness and depth of flavour that is truly distinctive.

Dubrovnik-style stuffed squid

This unique dish features tender squid stuffed with a flavourful mixture of breadcrumbs, garlic, parsley, and spices, then grilled or roasted to perfection. What sets Dubrovnik-style stuffed squid apart is the addition of local ingredients such as olive oil, Mediterranean herbs, and perhaps a splash of local wine or liqueur.

Rozata

Rozata is a luscious custard dessert that delights the senses with its creamy texture and delicate flavours. Similar to crème brûlée, rozata is made with eggs, sugar, milk, lemon zest, and rose water, giving it a subtle floral aroma and a hint of citrusy sweetness. The custard is baked until set, then chilled and topped with a caramel glaze before serving.

Dubrovnik-style marinated anchovies

Anchovies are a staple of Dubrovnik's seafood cuisine, and this dish showcases them in a unique and flavourful preparation. Fresh anchovies are marinated in a blend of olive oil, vinegar, garlic, and herbs, then left to cure for several hours or overnight.

Dubrovnik lemon sorbet

Refreshing and tangy, Dubrovnik lemon sorbet is the perfect palate cleanser or dessert on a hot summer day. Made with fresh lemon juice, sugar, and a splash of local liqueur, the sorbet is light, zesty, and bursting with citrus flavour. Served in chilled glasses or hollowed-out lemon halves, this icy treat is a refreshing way to cool off and enjoy the flavours of Dubrovnik's sun-drenched citrus groves.

Dubrovnik-style wild asparagus risotto

Wild asparagus is a prized ingredient in Dubrovnik's culinary repertoire, and this risotto showcases its delicate flavour and texture to perfection. The risotto is prepared with Arborio rice, homemade broth, white wine, and Parmesan cheese, then studded with tender wild asparagus spears.

Dubrovnik-style dried fig and almond tart

Figs and almonds are two of Dubrovnik's most beloved ingredients, and this tart combines them in a delightful dessert that is both rustic and elegant. The tart shell is filled with a mixture of dried figs, almonds, honey, and spices, then baked until golden and fragrant. Served warm with a scoop of vanilla ice cream or a drizzle of caramel sauce, this Dubrovnik fig and almond tart is a decadent treat that captures the essence of the Mediterranean.

Stuffed bell peppers

Stuffed bell peppers are a comforting and hearty dish that reflects the rustic flavours of Croatian home cooking. Bell peppers are filled with a savoury mixture of ground meat, rice, onions, garlic, and spices, then simmered in a rich tomato sauce until tender. The combination of sweet peppers, savoury filling, and aromatic sauce creates a symphony of flavours and textures that are sure to satisfy any appetite. Served with a side of creamy mashed potatoes or crusty bread, stuffed bell peppers are a classic comfort food in Dubrovnik.

Dubrovnik's culinary delights offer a journey of taste and tradition unlike any other. Whether you are savouring seafood by the sea or indulging in a hearty Dalmatian stew, each dish tells a story of the city's rich culinary heritage and vibrant gastronomic scene.

Unveiling Dubrovnik's secrets: Coastal charms revealed

Beyond the well-trodden paths of Dubrovnik's historic Old Town lie hidden treasures waiting to be discovered. From secluded beaches and secret viewpoints to tucked-away cafes and off-the-beaten-path attractions, these hidden gems offer a glimpse into the city's lesser-known corners and hidden delights. Let us embark on a journey to uncover the hidden gems of Dubrovnik and experience the city's charm from a different perspective.

Betina cave

Located along the rugged coastline near Dubrovnik, Betina Cave is a secluded gem known for its pristine waters and peaceful atmosphere. Accessible only by boat or by hiking along the rocky shoreline, this hidden spot offers a serene escape from the hustle and bustle of the city. Visitors can swim, snorkel, or simply relax on the rocky shores, surrounded by the beauty of the Adriatic Sea and the majestic cliffs that frame the cave.

Gradac park

Situated atop a hill overlooking Dubrovnik's Old Town, Gradac Park is a verdant oasis hidden from the bustling streets below. This hidden gem offers panoramic views of the city and the Adriatic Sea, making it the perfect spot for a leisurely stroll or a romantic picnic. Visitors can wander along shaded pathways, admire the colourful flora and fauna, and relax on secluded benches while taking in the breath-taking vistas.

Dubrovnik West pier

Away from the bustling streets of the Old Town lies the tranquil Dubrovnik West Pier, a hidden gem that offers stunning views of the Adriatic Sea and the city's ancient walls. This secluded spot is perfect for a leisurely stroll along the waterfront, watching the boats come and go, or simply soaking in the serenity of the sea breeze and the sound of lapping waves.

Croatian war of independence museum

Tucked away in the heart of Dubrovnik's Old Town, the Croatian War of Independence Museum offers a fascinating glimpse into the city's recent history. Housed in a historic building, the museum features exhibits and artifacts that tell the story of Dubrovnik's resilience during the 1991-1995 conflict. Visitors can explore underground bunkers, view documentary footage, and learn about the city's reconstruction efforts.

Fortress revelin

While Dubrovnik's city walls are a well-known attraction, Fortress Revelin offers a hidden alternative for stunning views of the city and the Adriatic Sea. Located on the eastern edge of the Old Town, this historic fortress is often overlooked by visitors, making it a peaceful retreat away from the crowds. Visitors can explore the well-preserved ramparts, climb the ancient staircases, and admire panoramic vistas of Dubrovnik's rooftops and the sparkling sea beyond.

Buza gate

Hidden within the labyrinthine streets of the Old Town, Buža Gate is a hidden gem that offers a glimpse into Dubrovnik's medieval past. This ancient gateway, dating back to the 15th century, was once a crucial entry point into the city. Today, it remains relatively undiscovered by tourists, making it a quiet and atmospheric spot to explore.

Sveti Jakov beach

Just a short walk from the Old Town lies Sveti Jakov Beach, a hidden gem beloved by locals and discerning travellers. Tucked away beneath towering cliffs, this secluded stretch of sand offers pristine waters and breath-taking views of Dubrovnik's skyline.

With its tranquil atmosphere and natural beauty, Sveti Jakov Beach is the perfect spot to escape the crowds and enjoy a relaxing day by the sea.

Dubrovnik city walls North entrance

While the main entrance to Dubrovnik's city walls is well-known, the North Entrance offers a quieter alternative for those seeking a more peaceful experience. Located near the Pile Gate, this hidden gem allows visitors to access the walls and explore at their own pace without the crowds.

Trsteno Arboretum

Tucked away along the coast north of Dubrovnik lies Trsteno Arboretum, a hidden gem that showcases centuries-old trees, lush gardens, and historic architecture. Founded in the 15th century, this botanical garden is one of the oldest in Croatia and offers a peaceful retreat from the hustle and bustle of the city. Visitors can wander through shaded pathways, admire exotic plant species, and relax in the tranquil surroundings of this hidden oasis.

Lokrum Island

Just a short boat ride from Dubrovnik's harbour lies Lokrum Island, a hidden paradise known for its lush vegetation, scenic walking trails, and tranquil beaches. This protected nature reserve offers a peaceful escape from the crowds, with secluded coves and rocky cliffs to explore. Visitors can wander through botanical gardens, visit historic landmarks such as the Benedictine monastery, or simply relax in the shade of pine trees overlooking the sparkling Adriatic Sea.

Dubrovnik's hidden gems offer a serene retreat from the hustle and bustle of the city, allowing visitors to connect with nature and experience the beauty of the Adriatic coast in peace. Whether you are seeking secluded beaches, panoramic viewpoints, or tranquil parks, these secret sanctuaries invite you to explore the quieter side of Dubrovnik and create unforgettable memories off the beaten path.

Adventure beckons: Exploring Dubrovnik's coastal playground

Dubrovnik's breath taking natural landscapes and pristine coastline offer a paradise for outdoor enthusiasts seeking adventure and exploration. From thrilling water sports to scenic hiking trails, the city and its surrounding areas provide endless opportunities to connect with nature and experience the beauty of the Adriatic coast.

City walls walk

Embarking on a walk along Dubrovnik's iconic city walls offers visitors a unique perspective of the Old Town's architectural marvels and panoramic vistas of the Adriatic Sea. Stretching over 1.2 miles (2 kilometres), the walls encircle the historic centre and provide glimpses into Dubrovnik's rich history, with strategically placed towers, forts, and gates. As you stroll atop the centuries-old fortifications, you'll be transported back in time, marvelling at the medieval charm of the city while capturing Instagram-worthy views of the terracotta rooftops and shimmering sea below.

Mount Srdj hike

Rising 1,352 feet (412 meters) above Dubrovnik, Mount Srdj beckons hikers with its scenic trails and panoramic viewpoints. The hike to the summit offers a rewarding challenge, winding through fragrant pine forests and rocky terrain. Upon reaching the peak, adventurers are treated to sweeping vistas of the city, Lokrum Island, and the Elaphiti Islands dotting the horizon.

Kayaking along the coastline

Exploring Dubrovnik's coastline by kayak provides a thrilling way to discover hidden gems along the Adriatic Sea. Paddling past towering cliffs and rocky shores, adventurers can access secluded coves, sea caves, and pristine beaches inaccessible by land. Guided tours offer insight into the region's marine ecosystems and local history, with opportunities for swimming, snorkelling, and cliff jumping along the way.

Snorkelling and scuba diving

Dubrovnik's crystal-clear waters beckon snorkelers and scuba divers to explore its vibrant underwater world, rich in marine life and hidden treasures. Snorkelling excursions offer the chance to swim alongside colourful fish, octopuses, and sea turtles in protected bays and marine reserves. For certified divers, Dubrovnik's dive sites boast ancient shipwrecks, underwater caves, and thriving coral reefs waiting to be explored.

Sailing excursions

Embarking on a sailing excursion from Dubrovnik allows travellers to explore the stunning Adriatic coastline and nearby islands at their own pace. Whether chartering a private yacht or joining a group tour, visitors can sail to secluded bays, swim in pristine waters, and soak up the Mediterranean sun aboard a luxury vessel.

Stand-up paddleboarding (SUP)

Stand-up paddleboarding has become increasingly popular in Dubrovnik, offering a unique way to explore the city's coastline and crystal-clear waters. Beginners can take lessons from experienced instructors before setting out to paddle along scenic routes, such as the tranquil waters of Lapad Bay or the rugged cliffs of Lokrum Island.

Rock climbing adventures

Adventure seekers can test their skills on Dubrovnik's rugged cliffs and limestone formations, which offer a variety of challenging routes for climbers of all levels. Guided rock-climbing tours provide instruction and equipment for climbers to ascend vertical walls and conquer breath-taking heights while enjoying panoramic views of the coastline.

Birdwatching excursions

Dubrovnik's diverse ecosystems and protected natural areas provide excellent opportunities for birdwatching enthusiasts to spot a wide variety of avian species. Guided birdwatching tours take visitors to scenic locations such as the Dubrovnik Riviera, where they can observe migratory birds, waterfowl, and raptors in their natural habitats. With knowledgeable guides leading the way, birdwatchers can learn about the region's birdlife while enjoying the tranquillity of nature and the beauty of Dubrovnik's coastal landscapes.

Zip-lining adventures

Experience an adrenaline rush with a zip-lining adventure through Dubrovnik's rugged landscape. Fly high above the treetops and soar across scenic valleys and canyons, enjoying panoramic views of the countryside and coastline below. With professional guides and state-of-the-art equipment, zip-lining offers a thrilling way to experience Dubrovnik's natural beauty and explore its hidden corners from a unique perspective.

Cave explorations

Delve into Dubrovnik's underground world with a cave exploration tour in nearby areas such as Konavle or the Pelješac Peninsula. Explore hidden caves, tunnels, and caverns formed by millennia of geological processes, and marvel at spectacular stalactites and stalagmites. Guided tours provide insight into the region's geological history and offer the chance to discover hidden gems deep beneath the surface.

From sea kayaking along the rugged coastline to hiking to scenic viewpoints, Dubrovnik's outdoor activities offer endless opportunities for adventure and exploration. Whether you are seeking adrenaline-pumping water sports or peaceful nature hikes, the city's natural beauty provides the perfect backdrop for unforgettable outdoor experiences.

Harbour of Traditions: Dubrovnik's vibrant festive scene

Dubrovnik's rich cultural heritage comes alive through its vibrant traditions and festivals, offering visitors a glimpse into the city's colourful past and lively present. From ancient customs rooted in centuries-old traditions to modern celebrations of art, music, and food, Dubrovnik's local festivals showcase the unique spirit and identity of this enchanting coastal city.

Dubrovački Karneval (February)

Dating back to the Middle Ages, the Dubrovnik Carnival is a lively celebration held in the weeks leading up to Lent. Festivities include colourful parades, masquerade balls, and street performances, with locals and visitors donning elaborate costumes and masks to join in the revelry. The carnival culminates in the burning of a symbolic effigy to mark the end of winter and the beginning of spring.

Svetkovina svetog Vlaha (February)

In addition to the Feast of Saint Blaise, Dubrovnik hosts a larger celebration every five years to commemorate the patron saint's miraculous protection of the city from invaders. The Festivity of Saint Blaise features grand religious ceremonies, cultural events, and historical re-enactments, drawing pilgrims and tourists from near and far to participate in the festivities.

Velika Gospa (August)

Celebrated on August 15th, the Feast of Assumption is a significant religious holiday in Dubrovnik, marking the Assumption of the Virgin Mary into heaven. The day begins with a solemn mass at the Dubrovnik Cathedral, followed by processions, feasting, and cultural performances throughout the city.

Veliki Petak (March/April)

On Good Friday, Dubrovnik hosts a solemn procession through the streets of the Old Town, re-enacting the Stations of the Cross and the Passion of Christ. Participants, dressed in traditional attire, carry statues and crosses as they follow the route marked by candlelight. The procession culminates at the Church of Saint Ignatius, where a prayer service is held, reflecting on the significance of Christ's sacrifice.

Dubrovački Jesenski Muzički Festival (September/October)

Music lovers flock to Dubrovnik in October for the Dubrovnik Autumn Music Festival, a showcase of classical music performed by renowned musicians from Croatia and around the world. Concerts take place in historic venues such as the Rector's Palace and the Dubrovnik Cathedral, providing an enchanting backdrop for chamber music, symphonies, and opera performances.

Dubrovačke Ljetne Igre (July/August)

The Dubrovnik Summer Festival is a month-long cultural extravaganza that transforms the city into a vibrant stage for theatre, music, dance, and art. Dating back to 1950, the festival showcases performances by international and Croatian artists in iconic venues such as the Rector's Palace, Lovrijenac Fortress, and Stradun street. Visitors can immerse themselves in the arts while experiencing the magic of summer nights in the enchanting Old Town, creating unforgettable memories of cultural exploration and entertainment.

Dubrovački Božićni Sajam (December)

During the holiday season, Dubrovnik comes alive with festive cheer at the annual Christmas Market. Set in the heart of the Old Town, the market features wooden stalls adorned with twinkling lights, offering handmade crafts, gifts, and traditional Croatian treats. Visitors can sip mulled wine, sample local delicacies, and browse for unique souvenirs while soaking in the festive atmosphere of Dubrovnik's enchanting streets.

Festa svetog Vlaha (February)

The Feast of Saint Blaise is one of Dubrovnik's oldest and most revered traditions, celebrating the city's patron saint with religious processions, folk music, and cultural rituals. On February 3rd, locals gather to honour Saint Blaise's miraculous protection of Dubrovnik from invaders, paying homage to the saint with prayers, blessings, and solemn ceremonies.

Dubrovački Međunarodni Filmski Festival (October)

The Dubrovnik International Film Festival celebrates the art of cinema with a diverse program of international and Croatian films, documentaries, and shorts. Held annually in late April or early May, the festival showcases screenings, workshops, and discussions in venues across the city, providing a platform for filmmakers and industry professionals to showcase their work and engage with audiences.

In conclusion, Dubrovnik's festivals provide a captivating glimpse into the city's rich heritage and vibrant culture. From ancient traditions to modern celebrations, each event adds depth to the tapestry of Dubrovnik's identity, inviting visitors to immerse themselves in its timeless charm and unforgettable experiences.

Seize the Moment: Dubrovnik's travel tips for adventurers

Dubrovnik, known as the 'Pearl of the Adriatic,' is a captivating destination steeped in history, culture, and natural beauty. Before embarking on your journey to this enchanting city, it is essential to familiarize yourself with some insider tips to make the most of your experience. From navigating the Old Town's cobblestone streets to sampling local cuisine and exploring hidden gems, these travel tips will help you create unforgettable memories in Dubrovnik.

Timing your visit

Planning your visit to Dubrovnik during the shoulder seasons of spring or autumn offers several advantages. Not only will you avoid the peak summer crowds and scorching temperatures, but you'll also experience milder weather ideal for exploring the city's outdoor attractions. Additionally, accommodation prices tend to be more affordable during these off-peak periods, allowing you to stretch your travel budget further and enjoy a more relaxed and authentic Dubrovnik experience.

Avoiding cruise ship crowds

Dubrovnik's popularity as a cruise ship destination can lead to overcrowding in the Old Town, especially during peak tourist season. To avoid the crowds, plan your visits to popular attractions such as the city walls and Stradun street early in the morning or late in the afternoon when cruise ship passengers are less likely to be ashore. Alternatively, explore off-the-beaten-path neighbourhoods and lesser-known sights to experience Dubrovnik's charm away from the tourist throngs.

Day trips and excursions

While Dubrovnik offers plenty to see and do within its city limits, do not miss the opportunity to explore the stunning landscapes and nearby islands on day trips and excursions. Visit the Elaphiti Islands for a day of island hopping and snorkelling, venture to the Pelješac Peninsula to sample local wines and oysters, or take a boat ride to Lokrum Island for a peaceful retreat surrounded by lush botanical gardens and secluded beaches.

Navigating transportation

Getting around Dubrovnik and its surrounding areas is relatively easy thanks to an efficient public transportation system. Consider purchasing a Dubrovnik Card, which provides unlimited access to city buses and discounts on attractions, or opt for taxis and rideshare services for convenient travel within the city. If you plan to explore the region independently, renting a car allows for flexibility and access to remote destinations, though parking in the Old Town can be limited and expensive.

Respecting local customs and etiquette

Dubrovnik has its own unique customs and etiquette that visitors should be aware of to show respect for the local culture. When visiting churches and religious sites, dress modestly and adhere to any posted guidelines regarding behaviour and photography. It is also customary to greet locals with a friendly 'dobar dan' (good day) or 'dobra večer' (good evening) and to wait for an invitation before entering someone's home.

Staying safe and secure

Dubrovnik is generally a safe destination for travellers, but it is essential to take precautions to ensure a secure visit. Keep valuables secure and be aware of pickpockets, especially in crowded areas like the Old Town and public transportation hubs. Stay hydrated and protected from the sun, especially during the hot summer months, and follow any local regulations and safety guidelines, particularly when engaging in water-based activities or exploring natural attractions.

Learning basic Croatian phrases

While many locals in Dubrovnik speak English and other languages, making an effort to learn basic Croatian phrases can enhance your travel experience and show respect for the local culture. Practice simple greetings, expressions of gratitude, and common phrases for ordering food and asking for directions. Locals appreciate visitors who attempt to communicate in their native language, fostering goodwill and cultural exchange during your time in Dubrovnik.

Exploring Dubrovnik's surroundings

While Dubrovnik's Old Town is undoubtedly captivating, do not overlook the city's surrounding areas. Take a scenic drive along the picturesque coastline to discover charming seaside villages, secluded beaches, and breath-taking viewpoints. Renting a kayak or paddleboard allows you to explore Dubrovnik's coastline from a different perspective, with opportunities to discover hidden caves, pristine coves, and crystal-clear waters.

Taking advantage of Dubrovnik card benefits

Purchasing a Dubrovnik Card offers more than just access to public transportation. The card provides discounts or free admission to many of Dubrovnik's top attractions, including museums, galleries, and historic sites. Additionally, holders of the Dubrovnik Card can skip the queues at popular tourist spots, saving both time and money while exploring the city's cultural treasures.

Capturing the perfect sunset

Dubrovnik is renowned for its spectacular sunsets, and there are plenty of vantage points from which to enjoy this daily spectacle. Head to the city walls or one of Dubrovnik's panoramic viewpoints, such as Mount Srđ or Fort Lovrijenac, to capture breath-taking views of the sun sinking below the horizon against the backdrop of the Adriatic Sea.

Embracing slow travel

Dubrovnik's timeless charm and laid-back atmosphere make it the perfect destination for slow travel. Instead of rushing from one attraction to the next, take the time to wander through the city's cobblestone streets, savouring the sights, sounds, and aromas of Dubrovnik's bustling markets, hidden alleyways, and historic landmarks. Slow down, relax, and allow yourself to fully appreciate the beauty and tranquillity of this enchanting Adriatic gem.

With these travel tips in mind, you are ready to embark on an unforgettable journey to Dubrovnik. Whether wandering the ancient streets of the Old Town, savouring local delicacies, or exploring the natural wonders of the surrounding region, Dubrovnik promises an immersive and unforgettable experience that will leave you enchanted and inspired.

Echoes of Dubrovnik: Coastal memories set adrift

As our journey through Dubrovnik draws to a close, take a moment to reflect on the myriad experiences and memories you've gathered in this enchanting city. From wandering the ancient streets of the Old Town to soaking in the breath-taking views from atop the city walls, Dubrovnik has left an indelible mark on your heart. As you bid farewell to its historic landmarks, vibrant culture, and warm hospitality, carry with you the echoes of laughter shared in bustling squares, the taste of freshly-caught seafood enjoyed in seaside taverns, and the sense of wonder inspired by its timeless beauty.

Though your time in Dubrovnik may be ending, the spirit of adventure and discovery ignited here will continue to accompany you on your travels. Whether you are reminiscing about sun-kissed afternoons spent exploring hidden alleys or dreaming of returning to witness the city's festivals and events, Dubrovnik will always hold a special place in your travel memories. As you venture onward to new destinations, may the magic of Dubrovnik stay with you, inspiring future adventures and reminding you of the endless wonders waiting to be explored.

Zadar: Harmonies of the Adriatic

Coastal bliss: Zadar's symphony of serenity

Nestled along Croatia's stunning Dalmatian coast, Zadar beckons travellers with its blend of ancient history, cultural richness, and breath-taking natural beauty. As you embark on your journey to this coastal gem, prepare to be captivated by its timeless charm and vibrant energy. From the historic cobblestone streets of the Old Town to the modern art installations along the waterfront, Zadar offers a tapestry of experiences waiting to be explored.

Steeped in over three millennia of history, Zadar boasts a legacy that spans civilizations, from the ancient Romans to the Venetian Republic and beyond. As you wander through its labyrinthine streets, you'll encounter a treasure trove of architectural marvels, including Roman ruins, medieval churches, and Venetian fortifications. But Zadar is not just a city frozen in time; it is a dynamic hub where past and present converge, inviting travellers to immerse themselves in its rich cultural tapestry while embracing the spirit of discovery that permeates its every corner.

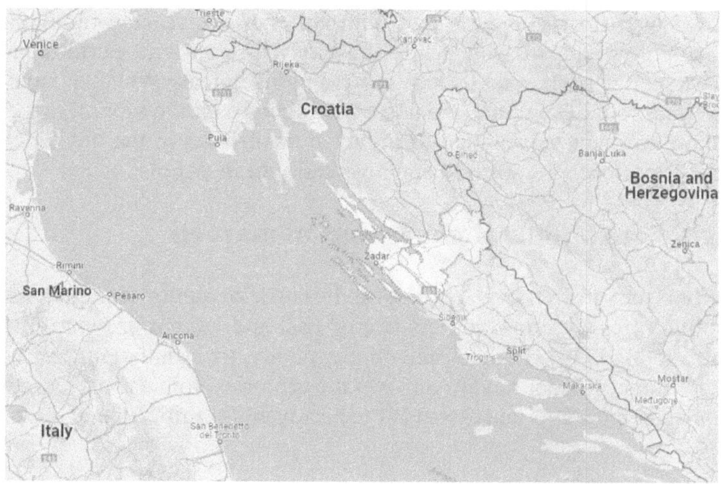

Zadar's ancient splendour: Echoes of Adriatic majesty

Zadar, steeped in a rich tapestry of history, stands as a testament to the enduring legacy of the civilizations that have left their mark upon its shores. With roots dating back to ancient times, Zadar has been shaped by the hands of many, from the Illyrians and Romans to the Byzantines and Venetians. Traces of its storied past can be found throughout the city, from the well-preserved Roman forum and ancient city walls to the majestic churches and palaces that dot its skyline.

One of Zadar's most iconic landmarks, the Roman Forum, stands as a testament to the city's ancient origins. Built in the 1st century BCE, this sprawling complex once served as the political, economic, and social heart of the Roman colony of Iader. Today, visitors can stroll through its ancient ruins, marvelling at the remnants of temples, basilicas, and other structures that once adorned this bustling civic centre. Beyond the Roman period, Zadar's history is punctuated by the influence of successive empires, including the Byzantine and Venetian eras, each leaving behind their own architectural and cultural legacies that continue to shape the city's identity today.

Navigating through time: Zadar's cultural odyssey

Zadar's local culture is a vibrant tapestry woven from centuries of tradition, creativity, and resilience. Rooted in the region's rich history and influenced by diverse cultural currents, the city's cultural identity is as dynamic as it is diverse. From the spirited folk music and dance traditions that echo through its streets to the lively markets and festivals that celebrate the bounty of the land and sea, Zadar's local culture reflects the resilience and resourcefulness of its people.

Music holds a special place in Zadar's cultural landscape, with the city renowned for its traditional folk music and modern-day music scene alike. Wander through the streets of the Old Town and you may stumble upon impromptu performances by local musicians, their melodies filling the air with the soul-stirring sounds of Dalmatian harmony. Art also flourishes in Zadar, with galleries showcasing the work of local painters, sculptors, and artisans, while the city's theatres and performance spaces provide a stage for both established and emerging talent. Whether savouring the flavours of traditional Dalmatian cuisine or engaging with the vibrant arts and music scene, visitors to Zadar are invited to immerse themselves in the city's rich cultural tapestry and experience the warmth and hospitality of its people.

Strolling through time: Zadar's coastal marvels

Zadar, a city steeped in history and culture, boasts a wealth of landmarks and points of interest that offer a glimpse into its storied past and vibrant present. From ancient Roman ruins to medieval churches and contemporary art installations, each landmark tells a unique story of Zadar's evolution over the centuries. Join us on a journey through the city's most iconic sights and discover the beauty and significance of these treasured landmarks.

Zadar cathedral

Dominating the city skyline with its majestic bell tower, Zadar Cathedral, also known as the Cathedral of St. Anastasia, is a sacred landmark that embodies the spiritual and architectural heritage of the city. Constructed in the 12th century in Romanesque style, the cathedral is dedicated to St. Anastasia, a revered Christian martyr. Its exterior features intricate stone carvings, while the interior is adorned with splendid frescoes, altarpieces, and religious artifacts dating back to the Middle Ages. Visitors can ascend the bell tower for panoramic views of Zadar's rooftops and surrounding landscapes, offering a glimpse into the city's medieval past and panoramic beauty.

The Forum

As the central hub of ancient Zadar, the Forum is a sprawling archaeological site that preserves the remnants of Roman civilization dating back to the 1st century BC. Surrounded by historic buildings and bustling with activity, the Forum served as the political, social, and economic heart of the city, hosting public gatherings, markets, and civic ceremonies. Today, visitors can explore the Forum's well-preserved ruins, including temples, columns, and a Roman forum, gaining insight into daily life in ancient Zadar and marvelling at its architectural splendour.

Five wells square

Five Wells Square is a historic square located in the heart of Zadar's Old Town, known for its distinctive architectural features and charming atmosphere. The square is named after five ornate wells built by the Venetians in the 16th century to provide the city with a reliable water supply during times of siege. Surrounded by Renaissance-era buildings and shaded by centuries-old trees, Five Wells Square is a popular gathering spot for locals and visitors alike, offering a tranquil escape from the bustling streets of the city.

Land gate

The Land Gate is a grandiose entrance to Zadar's Old Town, constructed in the 16th century as part of the city's defensive walls. Designed by the Venetian architect Michele Sanmicheli, the gate features a triumphal arch adorned with intricate reliefs and sculptures, symbolizing Zadar's resilience and prosperity. Above the gate, visitors can see the city's coat of arms and an inscription honouring the Venetian Republic. Passing through the Land Gate transports visitors back in time to an era of fortified cities and maritime empires, offering a glimpse into Zadar's storied past.

The sea organ

Designed by Croatian architect Nikola Bašić and inaugurated in 2005, the Sea Organ is an innovative architectural marvel located on Zadar's waterfront promenade. Consisting of 35 organ pipes embedded in marble steps, the organ harnesses the power of the sea's waves to create haunting melodies that echo along the coastline. Each pipe produces a unique sound depending on the size and force of the waves, offering visitors a mesmerizing auditory experience that changes with the tides.

St. Simeon's church

Nestled within Zadar's Old Town, St. Simeon's Church is a sacred sanctuary dedicated to St. Simeon, a revered Christian saint. Built in the 12th century in Romanesque style, the church is renowned for its beautiful facade adorned with intricate stone carvings and a magnificent rose window. Inside, visitors can marvel at the church's richly decorated interior, featuring Byzantine-style frescoes, marble altars, and a stunning golden reliquary containing the remains of St. Simeon.

The captain's tower

Situated on Zadar's waterfront, the Captain's Tower is a historic landmark that once served as part of the city's defensive fortifications. Built in the 13th century by the Venetians, the tower features a sturdy stone structure and a commanding position overlooking the harbour. Today, the Captain's Tower houses a maritime museum dedicated to Zadar's seafaring history, showcasing exhibits on navigation, shipbuilding, and maritime trade, offering visitors insight into the city's maritime heritage.

University of Zadar

The University of Zadar is a prestigious institution of higher learning located in the heart of the city. Founded in 1396, the university is one of the oldest in Europe and is renowned for its academic excellence and cultural significance. The university's historic campus features elegant courtyards, ornate buildings, and a richly decorated library housing rare manuscripts and scholarly works.

Arsenal

The Arsenal is a historic building located in Zadar's Old Town, originally constructed in the 16th century as a naval warehouse and shipyard. Today, the Arsenal serves as a cultural centre and exhibition space, hosting art exhibitions, concerts, and theatrical performances throughout the year. Visitors can admire the building's impressive architecture, with its grand arched entrances and Renaissance-style façade, and immerse themselves in Zadar's vibrant cultural scene by attending events held within its historic walls.

Queen Jelena Madijevka Park

Queen Jelena Madijevka Park is a scenic oasis located near Zadar's waterfront, offering a peaceful retreat from the hustle and bustle of the city. Named after Queen Jelena, the wife of King Dmitar Zvonimir, the park is adorned with lush greenery, colourful flower beds, and winding pathways that lead to picturesque viewpoints overlooking the Adriatic Sea.

In conclusion, Zadar's landmarks and points of interest paint a vivid portrait of its rich history, culture, and architectural legacy. From the ancient ruins of the Roman Forum to the innovative art installations along its waterfront, each site invites exploration and appreciation. As you bid farewell to this enchanting city, may the memories of its timeless beauty and enduring charm linger on, inspiring future adventures and discoveries.

Gastronomic sonata: Zadar's Culinary voyage along the Adriatic

Zadar, a coastal gem nestled on Croatia's Adriatic coast, offers a culinary journey that tantalizes the senses and reflects the region's rich gastronomic heritage. From fresh seafood caught daily in the azure waters of the Adriatic to aromatic herbs and spices sourced from the nearby Dalmatian hinterland, Zadar's culinary scene is a delightful blend of tradition and innovation.

Peka

Typically prepared outdoors over an open fire, peka involves slow-roasting a combination of meat, seafood, and vegetables in a cast-iron pot or baking dish, covered with a domed lid known as a peka. The ingredients are seasoned with olive oil, garlic, herbs, and sometimes wine or vinegar before being sealed and cooked to perfection over several hours.

Fritule

Fritule are irresistible bite-sized doughnuts that hold a special place in Croatian culinary tradition, particularly during festive occasions and celebrations. Made from a simple batter of flour, eggs, sugar, and milk, fritule are flavoured with grated lemon zest, a splash of rum, and sometimes plump raisins for added sweetness. The dough is deep-fried until golden and crispy, then dusted with powdered sugar for a delightful finishing touch.

Maraschino liqueur

Maraschino liqueur is a cherished spirit with roots dating back to the 16th century, when it was first produced in Zadar using Marasca cherries grown in the region. Distilled from the fruit, pits, and leaves of the Marasca cherry tree, Maraschino liqueur is renowned for its distinctive flavour profile, which balances the tartness of the cherries with notes of almond, vanilla, and floral aromas.

Brodetto di pesce

Brodetto di pesce, or fish broth, is a traditional seafood dish that showcases the bounty of the Adriatic Sea. Made with a variety of locally caught fish such as scorpionfish, sea bass, and bream, brodetto is simmered in a flavourful broth made from tomatoes, onions, garlic, white wine, and aromatic herbs. The result is a rich and fragrant stew with tender pieces of fish, perfect for dipping crusty bread and savouring the essence of the sea.

Rižot od kozica

Rižot od kozica, or shrimp risotto, is a comforting and indulgent dish that highlights the delicate flavour of Adriatic prawns. Arborio rice is cooked slowly with shallots, garlic, white wine, and fish stock until creamy and al dente, then topped with plump shrimp sautéed in olive oil and garlic. Finished with a sprinkle of fresh parsley and a squeeze of lemon juice, this creamy risotto is a culinary delight that celebrates the bounty of Zadar's coastal waters.

Brudet

Brudet is a beloved seafood stew that represents the essence of Dalmatian cuisine. Prepared with an array of fresh seafood such as fish, shellfish, and crustaceans, brudet is simmered slowly in a fragrant tomato-based sauce infused with garlic, onions, parsley, and local herbs. The slow cooking process allows the flavours to meld together, resulting in a hearty and comforting dish bursting with the essence of the Adriatic Sea. Served piping hot with a side of crusty bread for dipping into the rich broth, brudet is a culinary masterpiece that captures the soul of coastal Croatia.

Skampi na buzaru

Skampi na buzaru, or scampi in buzara sauce, is a classic Croatian seafood dish that showcases the natural sweetness of Adriatic langoustines. The langoustines are sautéed in olive oil with garlic, onions, and tomatoes, then simmered in white wine and flavoured with parsley, red pepper flakes, and a splash of brandy. The result is a fragrant and flavourful sauce that coats the tender langoustines, creating a dish that is both elegant and comforting.

Kroštule

Kroštule are traditional Croatian pastries that are often served during special occasions and holidays. Made from a simple dough of flour, eggs, sugar, and brandy, kroštule are rolled thin and cut into intricate shapes before being deep-fried until golden and crispy. Once fried, the pastries are dusted with powdered sugar or drizzled with honey for a touch of sweetness.

Ispod Peke

Ispod peke, or 'under the bell,' is a traditional method of cooking in Croatia that results in tender and flavourful dishes. Meat, typically lamb or veal, is marinated with garlic, rosemary, and olive oil, then placed in a clay pot with vegetables such as potatoes, carrots, and onions. The pot is covered with a metal or clay lid, then covered with hot coals and buried in the embers of a fire. After a few hours of slow cooking, the meat becomes incredibly tender and infused with the flavours of the marinade and vegetables, creating a truly unforgettable dining experience.

Crni Rizot

Crni rižot, or black risotto, is a classic Croatian dish made with cuttlefish or squid and black rice, giving it its distinctive colour. The rice is cooked slowly with onions, garlic, white wine, and fish or shellfish stock until creamy and tender, then finished with grated Parmesan cheese and a splash of olive oil. The rich and savoury flavours of the seafood and rice are complemented by the subtle sweetness of the onions and the tanginess of the wine, resulting in a dish that is as visually striking as it is delicious.

Bakalar na Bijelo

Bakalar na bijelo, or cod in white sauce, is a traditional Croatian dish that is often served during Lent and other religious holidays. Salted cod is soaked overnight to remove excess salt, then poached in milk until tender and flaky. The cod is then served with a creamy white sauce made from milk, flour, and butter, flavoured with garlic, parsley, and lemon zest. Served with boiled potatoes or crusty bread, bakalar na bijelo is a comforting and flavourful dish that is sure to warm the soul.

Fritto Misto di Mar

Fritto misto di mare, or mixed seafood fry, is a popular dish in coastal regions of Croatia that showcases the bounty of the Adriatic Sea. A variety of fresh seafood such as shrimp, squid, and small fish are lightly battered and fried until golden and crispy, then served with a squeeze of lemon and a sprinkle of sea salt.

In Zadar, culinary delights await at every turn, inviting visitors to savour the flavours of the Adriatic and experience the warmth and hospitality of Dalmatian cuisine. Whether indulging in fresh seafood by the waterfront or sampling traditional delicacies in cozy taverns tucked away in the city's historic streets, Zadar offers a culinary adventure that will leave a lasting impression on every palate.

Zadar's seaside whispers: Hidden delights await

In the heart of Croatia's Dalmatian Coast lies Zadar, a city brimming with hidden gems waiting to be unearthed by curious travellers. Beyond its well-known attractions, Zadar boasts a wealth of secrets tucked away in its narrow alleyways, historic squares, and picturesque corners. From secluded viewpoints offering panoramic vistas of the Adriatic to tucked-away cafes serving up authentic local cuisine, Zadar's hidden gems promise unforgettable experiences for those willing to explore off the beaten path. Join us as we embark on a journey to discover the lesser-known treasures that add depth and character to this enchanting coastal city.

Church of St. Simeon

Tucked away in a quiet corner of Zadar's Old Town, the Church of St. Simeon is a hidden architectural gem. Dating back to the 12th century, this Romanesque church features a stunning façade adorned with intricate carvings and a beautifully preserved interior, including a revered relic of St. Simeon.

Greeting to the sun installation

While the Sea Organ often steals the spotlight, Zadar's Greeting to the Sun Installation is a lesser-known marvel not to be missed. Designed by architect Nikola Bašić, this unique solar-powered installation consists of 300 multi-layered glass plates that light up in a mesmerizing display of colours at sunset, creating a magical atmosphere along the waterfront.

City walls walk

While many visitors flock to Zadar's Sea Organ and Greeting to the Sun, the City Walls Walk offers a quieter and equally rewarding experience. This hidden gem allows you to stroll along the ancient city walls, offering panoramic views of the Adriatic Sea, historic rooftops, and charming alleyways below.

Kalelarga

While Zadar's main thoroughfare, Kalelarga, may seem like a typical tourist hotspot, hidden gems await those who venture off the beaten path. Wander down the narrow side streets and alleys branching off from Kalelarga to discover hidden courtyards, local cafes, and artisan shops tucked away from the crowds.

Church of St. Donatus

Nestled amidst Zadar's historic centre, the Church of St. Donatus is a hidden gem of Romanesque architecture. Built in the 9th century, this circular church is renowned for its unique cylindrical shape and striking simplicity, making it a must-visit for architecture enthusiasts and history buffs alike.

Stomorica hill

For those seeking panoramic views away from the crowds, Stomorica Hill is a hidden gem worth exploring. Located just a short walk from the city centre, this tranquil hilltop offers stunning vistas of Zadar's skyline, surrounding islands, and the shimmering Adriatic Sea, providing the perfect spot for a peaceful retreat or sunset picnic.

Archaeological museum Zadar

While Zadar's Archaeological Museum may not be as well-known as its counterparts in larger cities, it houses a fascinating collection of artifacts that reveal the region's rich history. From Roman sculptures and medieval ceramics to ancient coins and artifacts from prehistoric times, this hidden gem offers valuable insights into Zadar's archaeological heritage.

Zadar's hidden gems offer a captivating blend of history, culture, and natural beauty, waiting to be discovered by intrepid travellers. From centuries-old churches and charming parks to innovative art installations and historic squares, these hidden treasures add depth and character to Zadar's enchanting landscape. Whether you are seeking solitude amidst ancient ruins or marvelling at modern art installations along the waterfront, Zadar's hidden gems promise unforgettable experiences off the beaten path.

Coastal escapades: Thrills amidst Zadar's historic wonders

As the sun-kissed jewel of Croatia's Adriatic coast, Zadar beckons outdoor enthusiasts with its myriad of exhilarating activities set against a backdrop of breath-taking natural beauty. From thrilling water sports to serene nature escapes, Zadar invites you to embark on unforgettable adventures that will leave you feeling invigorated and inspired.

Island hopping

Island hopping in Zadar allows you to explore the pristine beauty of the Adriatic Sea and its surrounding islands. From the vibrant island of Ugljan, known for its olive groves and picturesque villages, to the serene shores of Pašman, each island offers unique landscapes and cultural experiences. You can indulge in swimming in secluded bays, sunbathing on sandy beaches, and sampling local cuisine in charming waterfront restaurants.

Sea kayaking

Sea kayaking in Zadar is an exhilarating way to explore the region's rugged coastline and hidden sea caves. Paddle along crystal-clear waters, glide past dramatic cliffs, and venture into secluded coves accessible only by kayak. With experienced guides leading the way, you can discover hidden gems, such as the stunning Blue Cave on Biševo Island, and witness spectacular sunsets over the Adriatic horizon.

Hiking

Hiking in Zadar offers a rewarding experience amidst some of Croatia's most stunning natural landscapes, including Paklenica National Park and Velebit Mountain. Lace up your hiking boots and embark on a journey through lush forests, rocky gorges, and alpine meadows, following well-marked trails that cater to all levels of fitness and expertise.

Windsurfing and kiteboarding

Windsurfing and kiteboarding enthusiasts flock to Zadar's coastline to harness the power of the wind and waves in this adrenaline-pumping water sports. With favourable wind conditions and shallow, flatwater lagoons, Zadar offers ideal conditions for both beginners and experienced riders to practice their skills.

Rock climbing

Zadar's proximity to Paklenica National Park makes it a haven for rock climbing enthusiasts. The Park features limestone cliffs rising dramatically from the sea, offering a variety of routes suitable for climbers of all levels. Whether you are a beginner looking to hone your skills on easier routes or an experienced climber seeking a challenge on vertical walls, Paklenica has something for everyone.

Sailing

Set sail on the Adriatic Sea and experience the thrill of sailing in one of Europe's most beautiful sailing destinations. Whether you are an experienced sailor or a novice looking to learn the ropes, Zadar offers a range of sailing experiences to suit every preference. Charter a yacht or join a guided sailing tour to explore the hidden coves, secluded beaches, and picturesque islands that dot the coastline.

Birdwatching

Zadar's diverse ecosystems, including wetlands, forests, and coastal habitats, make it an excellent destination for birdwatching enthusiasts. Grab your binoculars and head to nature reserves such as Vransko Lake or Telašćica Nature Park to spot a variety of bird species, including herons, eagles, flamingos, and migratory birds. Join guided birdwatching tours led by knowledgeable local guides who can help you identify different species and share insights into their behaviour and habitats.

Stand-up paddleboarding (SUP)

Glide across the tranquil waters of the Adriatic Sea on a stand-up paddleboard (SUP) adventure in Zadar. SUP allows you to explore the coastline at your own pace, paddling along scenic shores, and exploring hidden coves and sea caves. With calm waters and stunning views of the surrounding islands, Zadar provides the perfect backdrop for a relaxing and enjoyable SUP experience.

Snorkelling

Discover the vibrant underwater world of the Adriatic Sea through snorkelling in Zadar. With its crystal-clear waters and rich marine biodiversity, Zadar offers excellent snorkelling opportunities for enthusiasts of all ages and skill levels. Slip on your mask, snorkel, and fins, and explore colourful coral reefs, rocky seascapes, and schools of tropical fish.

Beach volleyball

Enjoy a game of beach volleyball on Zadar's sandy shores, where the sun, sea, and sand create the perfect setting for outdoor fun and friendly competition. Gather your friends or join a pickup game with locals and visitors alike, spiking and diving in the soft sand as you soak up the coastal ambiance. With numerous beach volleyball courts scattered along Zadar's beaches, including Borik and Kolovare, you can enjoy the thrill of the game and the refreshing sea breeze all year round.

Zip-lining

Experience the thrill of soaring through the air on a zip-lining adventure in Zadar's stunning countryside. Strap into a harness, take a deep breath, and launch yourself across the treetops, flying high above lush forests and scenic valleys. With exhilarating zip-line courses available in nearby destinations such as Biograd na Moru and Maslenica, you can unleash your inner adventurer and enjoy panoramic views of the Adriatic landscape from a whole new perspective.

Whether you are seeking adrenaline-pumping thrills or peaceful moments in nature, Zadar's outdoor activities offer something for everyone. From kayaking along the coastline to hiking through scenic trails, each adventure promises unforgettable memories and a deeper connection to the natural beauty of this enchanting region.

Festive reverie: Zadar's Coastal celebrations and traditions

Zadar's cultural tapestry is woven with a rich array of traditions and festivals, each offering a glimpse into the city's storied past and vibrant present. From musical marvels to culinary delights, these local celebrations reflect the spirit and identity of the community, inviting visitors to immerse themselves in the unique rhythm of Zadar's cultural life.

Fešta sv. Donata (August)

Fešta sv. Donata celebrates the patron saint of Zadar, St. Donatus, with a series of events held in and around the iconic St. Donatus Church. The festival typically includes religious processions, solemn Masses, and concerts featuring classical and sacred music performed by local and international artists. Visitors can also explore exhibitions and guided tours focusing on the history and architecture of the church, as well as enjoy traditional Croatian cuisine served at outdoor food stalls.

Sv. Krševan (November)

The Sv. Krševan Festival commemorates St. Krševan, the patron saint of Zadar, with a week-long celebration filled with religious devotion and cultural festivities. The highlight of the festival is the solemn procession through the streets of Zadar, where locals dressed in traditional attire carry statues of St. Krševan and other saints, accompanied by clergy and marching bands.

Noć punog miseca (July/August)

Noć punog miseca, or Night of the Full Moon, is a magical event that takes place during the full moon cycle in Zadar. This enchanting evening is celebrated with a variety of activities and cultural events, including moonlit guided tours of the city's historic landmarks, outdoor film screenings under the stars, and live music performances in scenic locations. Visitors can also participate in yoga and meditation sessions held on the beach, or enjoy moonlit boat cruises along the Adriatic coast.

Šušur (July/August)

Šušur, also known as the Zadar Summer Festival, is a vibrant cultural event that takes place during the summer months, showcasing the city's rich artistic heritage and contemporary creativity. The festival features a diverse program of music concerts, theatre performances, art exhibitions, and street performances, held in various venues throughout Zadar's historic centre. Visitors can immerse themselves in the lively atmosphere of Šušur, enjoying open-air concerts in picturesque squares, theatrical productions in ancient ruins, and art installations in modern galleries.

Festival Dalmatinskih Klapa (July)

The Festival Dalmatinskih Klapa celebrates the traditional a cappella singing style known as klapa, which originated in the Dalmatian region of Croatia. This annual festival brings together klapa singing groups from across Croatia and beyond to perform in Zadar's historic squares and venues. Audiences can enjoy soulful harmonies, heartfelt lyrics, and lively performances that celebrate the rich musical heritage of Dalmatia. In addition to concerts and recitals, the festival often includes workshops and seminars on klapa singing, providing a platform for enthusiasts to learn about and engage with this beloved musical tradition.

Maškare (February/March)

Maškare, or Carnival, is a festive celebration held in the weeks leading up to Lent, marking the end of winter and the beginning of spring. During Maškare, Zadar's streets come alive with colourful parades, elaborate costumes, and lively music, as locals and visitors alike join in the revelry. Participants don masks and costumes representing characters from folklore and popular culture, dancing and singing their way through the city's squares and streets.

Dan Grada (November)

Dan Grada, or City Day, is an annual celebration held on December 5th to commemorate the founding of Zadar and honour its rich history and cultural heritage. The day begins with a solemn Mass at the city's cathedral, followed by a procession through the streets led by local officials and dignitaries. Throughout the day, various cultural and artistic events take place, including concerts, exhibitions, and theatre performances, showcasing Zadar's vibrant cultural scene.

Festa od Gusta (September)

Festa od Gusta, or the Taste Festival, is a culinary extravaganza that celebrates the rich gastronomic heritage of Zadar and the surrounding region. Held in the city's main squares and waterfront promenades, the festival showcases a wide range of local delicacies, from fresh seafood and olive oil to artisanal cheeses and wines. Visitors can sample dishes prepared by top chefs from Zadar's renowned restaurants, attend cooking demonstrations and workshops, and purchase gourmet products from local producers.

Ribarska Noć (July/August)

Ribarska Noć, or Fishermen's Night, is an annual celebration of Zadar's maritime heritage and the importance of fishing to the local economy. The event takes place in the city's harbour, where fishing boats are decorated with colourful lights and festive decorations. Visitors can enjoy live music performances, dance to traditional Dalmatian tunes, and feast on freshly caught seafood prepared in various ways. Street vendors sell grilled fish, octopus salad, and other seafood specialties, while local artisans showcase their handcrafted goods.

Sveta Lucija (December)
Sveta Lucija, or St. Lucy's Day, is celebrated on December 13th in honour of St. Lucy, the patron saint of eyesight and light. In Zadar, the day is marked by a traditional procession through the city's streets, led by young girls dressed in white robes and wreaths of candles. The procession culminates in a Mass at St. Lucy's Church, where prayers are offered for the protection of eyesight and the blessings of light.

As the sun sets on another year of festivities, the spirit of Zadar's traditions and festivals continues to resonate, weaving together the threads of community, heritage, and creativity. Whether experiencing the haunting melodies of the Sea Organ or savouring the flavours of the Fešta od Škampi, these cultural treasures leave an indelible mark on the hearts of all who partake, fostering a deeper connection to the soul of Zadar.

Coastal charms unravelled: Insider tips for exploring Zadar

With its ancient history, breath-taking natural landscapes, and vibrant cultural scene, Zadar offers a truly immersive experience for travellers seeking authenticity and adventure. From exploring historic landmarks to savouring local delicacies, there is something magical waiting to be discovered around every corner.

Currency exchange

While many places in Zadar accept credit cards, it is always advisable to carry some cash for smaller purchases and transactions, especially in local markets, cafes, and smaller establishments. Currency exchange offices can be found throughout the city, including at the airport, main bus station, and in tourist areas. Before exchanging your currency, compare rates to ensure you are getting the best deal, and be aware of any fees or commissions charged by the exchange bureau. Additionally, consider withdrawing cash from ATMs using your debit card, but be mindful of potential withdrawal fees and exchange rates.

Local transportation

Zadar offers an efficient and affordable public transportation system consisting of buses and ferries, making it easy to explore the city and its surrounding areas. Purchase a Zadar Card, available at tourist information centres and kiosks, which provides unlimited access to public buses and discounts on admission to museums, galleries, and attractions. Bus routes are well-marked, with schedules available online or at bus stops, and ferries operate regularly to nearby islands and coastal destinations.

Stay hydrated

Zadar enjoys a Mediterranean climate characterized by hot summers, so it is essential to stay hydrated, especially when spending time outdoors or exploring the city's historic sites. Carry a refillable water bottle with you and take advantage of public water fountains, which are available in parks, squares, and along the waterfront. Many cafes and restaurants also offer complimentary tap water, so do not hesitate to ask for a refill when dining out. Avoid excessive alcohol consumption, which can contribute to dehydration, and seek shade during the hottest parts of the day to prevent overheating.

Respect cultural norms

While Zadar is a welcoming and cosmopolitan city, it is important to respect local customs and traditions to ensure a positive and enjoyable experience for both visitors and residents. When visiting religious sites such as churches or monasteries, dress modestly and cover your shoulders and knees out of respect for religious sensitivities. In public spaces, avoid loud or disruptive behaviour, especially late at night or in residential areas, to maintain the tranquillity of the city.

Explore off the beaten path

While Zadar's main attractions are undoubtedly impressive, do not be afraid to venture off the beaten path and discover hidden gems tucked away in the city's quieter neighbourhoods. Wander through the labyrinthine streets of the Old Town, where you'll stumble upon charming cafes, boutique shops, and hidden courtyards waiting to be explored. Take a leisurely stroll along the Riva promenade or explore the vibrant markets of Kalelarga Street, immersing yourself in the local atmosphere and discovering Zadar's lesser-known treasures.

Safety precautions

Zadar is generally a safe destination for travellers, but it is always wise to take basic safety precautions to protect yourself and your belongings. Keep your valuables secure and be mindful of pickpockets in crowded areas, especially during peak tourist seasons. Avoid walking alone in poorly lit or secluded areas at night, and trust your instincts if you feel uncomfortable in any situation. Familiarize yourself with emergency numbers and the location of the nearest police stations and medical facilities.

Seasonal considerations

Zadar experiences distinct seasons, with summer being the most popular time to visit due to its warm weather and sunny skies. However, peak season also means larger crowds and higher prices, so consider visiting during the shoulder seasons of spring and autumn for fewer tourists and more affordable accommodations. Winter offers a quieter atmosphere, with the added bonus of festive holiday markets and cultural events.

Environmental responsibility

As a responsible traveller, strive to minimize your environmental impact during your stay in Zadar. Choose eco-friendly accommodations that prioritize sustainability and conservation efforts, such as hotels with energy-efficient practices or eco-lodges

powered by renewable energy sources. Reduce waste by opting for reusable items like water bottles, shopping bags, and utensils, and dispose of trash responsibly in designated bins. Respect wildlife and natural habitats when exploring outdoor areas, and follow Leave No Trace principles to preserve Zadar's pristine landscapes for future generations to enjoy.

Sun protection

Zadar enjoys abundant sunshine throughout the year, especially during the summer months. Protect yourself from the sun's harmful rays by wearing sunscreen with a high SPF, a wide-brimmed hat, and sunglasses. Seek shade during the hottest part of the day, typically between 10 am and 4 pm, to avoid sunburn and heat exhaustion. If you plan to spend time at the beach, bring along a beach umbrella or sunshade for added protection.

Language apps and maps

Before you arrive in Zadar, download language translation apps and offline maps to your smartphone to assist you during your travels. These tools can be invaluable for communicating with locals, navigating the city's streets, and accessing useful information about attractions, restaurants, and public transportation options. Make sure to download the necessary data or offline maps while you have Wi-Fi access to avoid data charges or connectivity issues later on.

Emergency preparedness

While Zadar is a safe destination for travellers, it is essential to be prepared for any unforeseen emergencies. Carry a copy of your passport, travel insurance information, and emergency contacts with you at all times, and store electronic copies securely in cloud storage or email them to yourself for easy access. Familiarize yourself with the location of the nearest embassy or consulate in case you need assistance while abroad. Additionally, consider purchasing travel insurance that covers medical emergencies, trip cancellations, and other unexpected events.

With its wealth of attractions and diverse experiences, Zadar promises a memorable getaway for travellers seeking history, culture, and natural beauty. By following these travel tips, you'll uncover the city's secrets, savour its culinary delights, and create lasting memories of your time in this enchanting destination.

Adieu to Zadar's coastal enchantment: Memories set adrift

As the sun sets on your time in Zadar, it is impossible not to feel a sense of gratitude for the moments of wonder and discovery this city has bestowed upon you. From wandering the ancient streets to basking in the warmth of its welcoming culture, Zadar has woven itself into the fabric of your journey, leaving an indelible mark on your soul. As you prepare to bid farewell to its cobblestone alleys and bustling squares, take a moment to cherish the memories you've created and the connections you've forged with its people.

But as one chapter ends, another begins, and the spirit of Zadar will continue to guide you on your travels. Whether you find yourself reminiscing about the melodies of its

music or yearning to return to its sun-drenched shores, know that Zadar will always hold a special place in your heart. As you venture forth into the world, may the lessons learned and experiences gained in Zadar serve as a beacon of inspiration, reminding you to embrace the beauty of every moment and the richness of every encounter along the way.

Hvar: Lavender scented bliss

Vibrant tapestry: Immersing in Hvar's Local Culture

Nestled in the azure waters of the Adriatic Sea, Hvar emerges as a gem of the Dalmatian coast, captivating visitors with its pristine beauty and rich heritage. Renowned as one of Croatia's most idyllic islands, Hvar beckons travellers with its sun-drenched beaches, fragrant lavender fields, and charming medieval towns. As you step foot on this enchanting island, you'll be transported to a world where ancient history mingles with modern luxury, offering an unforgettable blend of relaxation and adventure.

With its sun-kissed shores and vibrant cultural scene, Hvar has long been a haven for artists, poets, and wanderers seeking inspiration and serenity. From the bustling streets of Hvar Town to the tranquil vineyards of Stari Grad, the island exudes a timeless allure that captivates all who visit. Whether you are savouring fresh seafood at a waterfront taverna, exploring hidden coves on a sailing excursion, or simply basking in the warmth of the Mediterranean sun, Hvar invites you to experience the essence of island life in all its splendour.

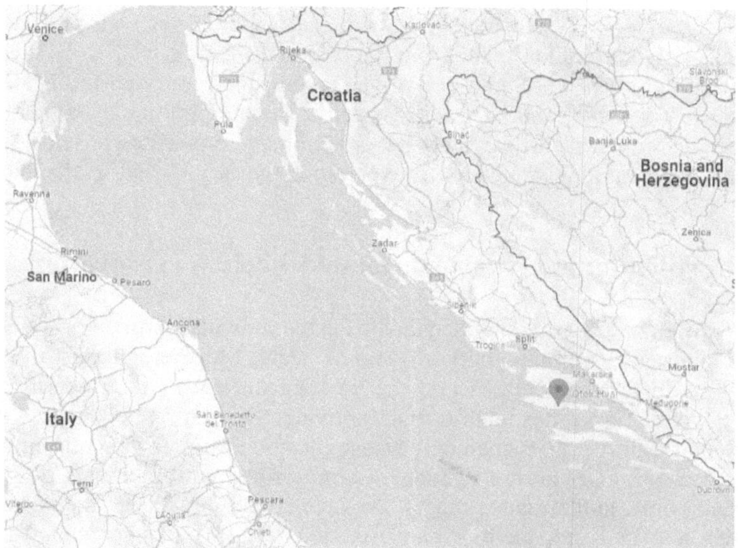

Footprints of time: Hvar's storied historical narrative

Hvar, steeped in centuries of history, bears the traces of its illustrious past in every corner of the island. From its ancient Greek roots to its medieval fortresses and Renaissance architecture, Hvar stands as a living testament to the diverse civilizations that have shaped its identity over the ages. One of the island's most iconic landmarks is the imposing Fortica Španjola, perched high above Hvar Town, which offers panoramic views of the Adriatic Sea and serves as a reminder of the island's strategic importance throughout history.

In addition to its fortifications, Hvar boasts a wealth of historical sites that offer insights into its storied past. Wander through the narrow streets of Stari Grad, the oldest continuously inhabited settlement in Croatia, and discover remnants of its Greek, Roman, and Venetian heritage. Visit the 13th-century Franciscan Monastery, home to a rich collection of art and artifacts, or explore the picturesque village of Vrboska, known as 'Little Venice' for its charming canal system. With each step, you'll uncover layers of history that have shaped Hvar into the captivating destination it is today.

Community chronicles: Unveiling Hvar's cultural identity

Hvar's vibrant local culture is a mosaic of traditions, customs, and influences that have been passed down through generations, enriching the island's identity. At the heart of Hvar's cultural tapestry is its deep-rooted connection to the sea, reflected in the islanders' way of life, cuisine, and folklore. Fishing has long been a vital part of Hvar's economy, and the annual Fishermen's Nights celebration pays homage to this maritime heritage with music, dancing, and feasting on freshly caught seafood.

Throughout the year, Hvar comes alive with a calendar of festivals and events that celebrate its rich cultural heritage. From the solemn processions of Holy Week to the lively festivities of the Hvar Summer Festival, visitors have the opportunity to immerse themselves in the island's unique traditions and customs. Traditional Dalmatian music and dance performances, artisan markets, and culinary showcases provide a window into Hvar's soul, inviting travellers to experience the island's authentic charm first-hand.

Sights of splendour: Hvar's landmarks beckon exploration

As you step foot onto Hvar's shores, you'll be greeted by the warm embrace of its sun-drenched landscapes and the gentle rhythm of island life. Here, amidst the timeless beauty of its historic landmarks and the bustling energy of its modern cafes and boutiques, you'll find a destination that captivates the senses and ignites the soul. Whether you are drawn to its ancient fortresses, its picturesque vineyards, or its idyllic beaches, Hvar promises an unforgettable journey filled with moments of discovery, delight, and pure Mediterranean magic. So, take a deep breath, let the island's spirit wash over you, and prepare to embark on a voyage of wonder and wanderlust. Welcome to Hvar, where every moment is an invitation to explore, indulge, and savour the beauty of life.

Hvar theatre

Dating back to the 17th century, the Hvar Theatre is one of the oldest public theatres in Europe. Nestled in the heart of Hvar Town, this historic theatre hosts a variety of performances, including plays, concerts, and cultural events, offering visitors a glimpse into Hvar's theatrical heritage.

Hvar cathedral

Dominating the skyline of Hvar Town, the Cathedral of St. Stephen is a striking landmark known for its elegant Renaissance architecture and towering bell tower. Inside, visitors can admire stunning artworks, intricate carvings, and the exquisite marble altars, offering a glimpse into Hvar's religious and artistic heritage.

Spanjola fortress

Located on the hill above Hvar Town, Spanjola Fortress offers sweeping views of the Adriatic Sea and the surrounding islands. Originally built in the 16th century to defend against pirates, the fortress now houses a museum showcasing Hvar's maritime history and archaeological artifacts.

Hvar fortress

Perched high above the town of Hvar, the historic fortress offers panoramic views of the surrounding islands and coastline. Dating back to the 16th century, this impressive fortress is a must-visit for history enthusiasts and offers insight into Hvar's strategic importance throughout the centuries.

Franciscan monastery

Tucked away on the western edge of Hvar Town, the Franciscan Monastery is a serene retreat renowned for its peaceful cloister, tranquil gardens, and centuries-old olive groves. Founded in the 15th century, the monastery's museum houses a valuable collection of medieval artifacts, religious relics, and works of art, providing insight into Hvar's cultural and spiritual traditions.

Hvar town square

Immerse yourself in the lively ambiance of Hvar Town Square, the heart of the island's social and cultural life. Admire the elegant architecture of the surrounding buildings, enjoy a leisurely coffee at one of the charming cafes, and soak up the vibrant atmosphere as locals and visitors mingle in this picturesque setting.

St. Stephen's square

Wander through St. Stephen's Square, a charming plaza lined with cafes, shops, and historic buildings. Admire the impressive Renaissance architecture of the Hvar Cathedral and soak up the Mediterranean ambiance as you explore this bustling town centre.

Fortica fortress

Perched atop a hill overlooking Hvar Town, Fortica Fortress, also known as Španjol, offers panoramic views of the Adriatic Sea and the neighbouring islands. Built in the 16th century to defend against invaders, the fortress now houses a museum showcasing Hvar's military history, ancient weaponry, and archaeological treasures, providing visitors with a glimpse into the island's storied past.

Pakleni Islands

Just off the coast of Hvar, the Pakleni Islands are a pristine archipelago of secluded coves, crystal-clear waters, and lush Mediterranean vegetation. Whether you are seeking a quiet spot to relax or an adventurous day of snorkelling and diving, the Pakleni Islands offer endless opportunities for exploration and discovery.

As you conclude your journey through Hvar, take a moment to reflect on the memories you've made and the sights you've seen. Whether you've immersed yourself in the island's rich history, embraced its lively atmosphere, or simply savoured its tranquil beauty, Hvar has left an indelible mark on your soul. As you bid farewell to this enchanting island, carry with you the spirit of Hvar and the promise of future adventures. Until we meet again, may the memories of Hvar continue to inspire and delight you.

Taste of tradition: Savoury delights of Hvar's cuisine

From fresh seafood caught daily to locally sourced produce bursting with flavour, Hvar's culinary delights offer a tantalizing journey for the taste buds. Whether you are indulging in traditional Dalmatian cuisine or savouring international flavours with a local twist, Hvar promises a culinary experience that celebrates the island's rich gastronomic heritage and the bounty of the Adriatic Sea

Lavender honey

Harvested from the fragrant fields of lavender that blanket the island, Hvar's lavender honey is a sweet nectar with a delicate floral aroma. This golden-hued honey captures the essence of the island's lavender blooms, offering a subtle yet distinct flavour that pairs perfectly with fresh bread, cheese, or drizzled over Greek yogurt.

Octopus peka

A beloved dish of Hvar, Octopus Peka is a culinary masterpiece that reflects the island's maritime heritage. Tender octopus is marinated in olive oil, garlic, and

Mediterranean herbs before being slow-cooked under a bell-shaped lid, known as a peka, over an open fire.

Black risotto

A culinary gem of Dalmatia, Hvar's black risotto is a testament to the island's rich seafood tradition. Made with locally caught cuttlefish and their ink, along with Arborio rice, garlic, onions, and olive oil, this velvety dish is as visually striking as it is delicious.

Dalmatian prosciutto

Hvar's Dalmatian prosciutto is a delicacy cherished for its exceptional quality and flavour. Crafted from locally raised pork, the ham is carefully salted and air-dried, then aged for months to develop its distinctive taste and texture. Sliced paper-thin and served alongside freshly baked bread, olives, and local cheeses, Dalmatian prosciutto is a true taste of Hvar's culinary heritage.

Grilled Adriatic fish

Hvar's crystal-clear waters teem with a variety of fish, making seafood an integral part of the island's cuisine. Grilled Adriatic fish is a simple yet delectable dish that highlights the freshness and quality of the local catch. Whole fish, such as sea bass or bream, are seasoned with olive oil, garlic, and Mediterranean herbs, then grilled to perfection over an open flame.

Black truffle pasta

Hvar's black truffles are a prized treasure found in the island's lush forests. Paired with handmade pasta, this dish is a luxurious indulgence for food enthusiasts. The earthy aroma and intense flavour of the truffles infuse the pasta, creating a dish that is rich, savoury, and utterly satisfying. Topped with grated Parmesan cheese and fresh herbs, black truffle pasta is a culinary masterpiece that showcases Hvar's natural bounty.

Hvar lamb peka

Peka is a traditional Croatian cooking method that involves slow-roasting meat and vegetables in a covered pot over hot coals. Hvar lamb peka is a rustic yet refined dish that showcases the island's tender, flavourful lamb. Marinated with garlic, rosemary, and olive oil, the lamb is cooked low and slow until it is melt-in-your-mouth tender, while potatoes and vegetables absorb the rich flavours of the meat and juices.

Almond cake with orange blossom syrup

Hvar's almond cake with orange blossom syrup is a delightful dessert that captures the essence of the island's Mediterranean flavours. Made with ground almonds, eggs, and sugar, the cake is moist, nutty, and subtly sweet. It is then soaked in a fragrant syrup made from orange blossom water, sugar, and lemon juice, infusing it with a delicate floral aroma and citrusy tang.

Stuffed squid

Stuffed squid is a traditional Dalmatian dish that is popular in Hvar. Fresh squid are filled with a savoury mixture of breadcrumbs, garlic, parsley, and olive oil, then grilled or baked until tender and golden brown. The squid are served hot off the grill, drizzled with lemon juice and accompanied by a side of boiled potatoes or a fresh salad.

Figs with goat cheese and prosciutto

Hvar's sun-kissed figs are celebrated for their sweet, luscious flavour and vibrant purple hue. When paired with creamy goat cheese and savoury prosciutto, they create a harmonious balance of flavours and textures. Fresh figs are sliced in half and filled with tangy goat cheese, then wrapped in thinly sliced prosciutto to create a delightful appetizer or light snack.

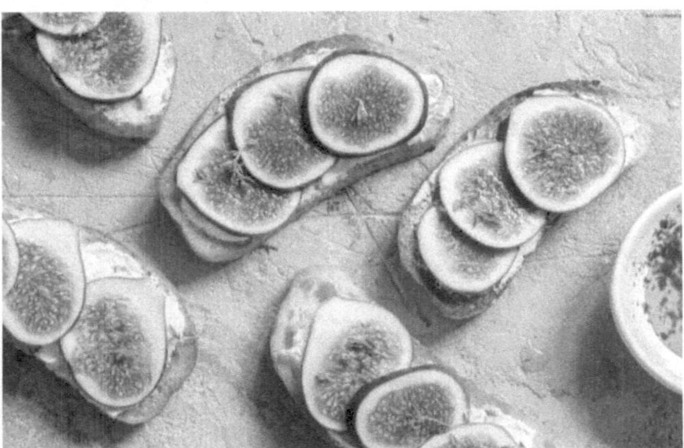

As you explore Hvar's culinary delights, each bite tells a story of tradition, innovation, and the rich flavours of the Adriatic. From the earthy notes of locally grown herbs to the salty tang of the sea, Hvar's cuisine is a celebration of life, love, and the bounty of nature. So, take a seat at the table, raise a glass of local wine, and savour every moment of your gastronomic journey through this enchanting island paradise.

Off-the-beaten path: Unveiling Hvar's hidden delights

Beyond the well-trodden paths and bustling squares lies a world of hidden treasures waiting to be discovered in Hvar. These hidden gems, tucked away in secret corners and secluded spots, offer a glimpse into the island's lesser-known wonders and provide intrepid travellers with unforgettable experiences off the beaten track.

Malo grablje

Nestled in the hills above Hvar Town, Malo Grablje is a charming abandoned village frozen in time. Its stone houses, overgrown vineyards, and winding pathways evoke a sense of nostalgia and mystery, inviting visitors to wander through its deserted streets and uncover its forgotten stories.

Velo grablje

Just a short drive from Hvar Town, Velo Grablje is a picturesque hamlet known for its terraced vineyards, olive groves, and panoramic views of the Adriatic Sea. Visitors can explore its ancient stone houses, sample local wines and olive oils, and immerse themselves in the timeless beauty of rural Hvar.

Stiniva bay

Tucked away on the southern coast of the island, Stiniva Bay is a hidden gem accessible only by boat or by a challenging hike down a steep trail. Enclosed by towering cliffs and surrounded by azure waters, this secluded beach offers a tranquil escape from the crowds and a pristine setting for swimming, snorkelling, and sunbathing.

Pokrivenik cove

Tucked away on the northern coast of Hvar, Pokrivenik Cove is a hidden gem accessible only by boat or a rugged hiking trail. With its secluded pebble beach, crystal-clear waters, and surrounding pine forests, Pokrivenik offers a serene escape from the crowds and a perfect spot for swimming, snorkelling, and picnicking in nature's embrace.

Sveta Nedjelja

Perched on the cliffs overlooking the Adriatic Sea, Sveta Nedjelja is a picturesque village renowned for its scenic beauty and traditional charm. Visitors can explore its narrow streets, visit the historic church of St. Nicholas, and enjoy stunning views of the coastline from its cliffside promenade.

Naplovac beach

Situated on the southern coast of Hvar near the village of Milna, Naplovac Beach is a hidden paradise nestled between rocky cliffs and lush Mediterranean vegetation. Accessible via a short hike through olive groves and vineyards, this secluded beach rewards visitors with its pristine beauty, calm turquoise waters, and panoramic views of the Adriatic Sea.

Grapceva cave

Located inland from Hvar Town, Grapceva Cave is an ancient archaeological site dating back thousands of years. This hidden gem offers a fascinating glimpse into prehistoric life on the island, with its intricate cave formations, mysterious rock carvings, and evidence of early human habitation. Guided tours are available for visitors interested in exploring this unique underground world.

Milna bay

Nestled on the southern coast of Hvar, Milna Bay is a hidden harbour surrounded by rugged cliffs and lush greenery. Away from the hustle and bustle of the main tourist areas, Milna exudes a peaceful atmosphere and offers a tranquil setting for swimming, sunbathing, and enjoying the natural beauty of the island.

Kabal peninsula

Situated on the northern coast of Hvar, the Kabal Peninsula is a hidden gem characterized by its rugged cliffs, hidden coves, and untouched natural beauty. Accessible via a scenic hiking trail from the town of Hvar, the peninsula offers spectacular views of the Adriatic Sea and is a paradise for outdoor adventurers and nature lovers.

Dubovica beach

Accessible only by a narrow footpath or by boat, Dubovica Beach is a hidden oasis of tranquillity on the southern coast of Hvar. With its crystal-clear waters, pebble shores, and dramatic cliffs, this secluded cove offers a secluded retreat for sunbathers, swimmers, and nature lovers seeking solitude and serenity.

As you venture off the beaten path and explore the hidden gems of Hvar, you'll discover a world of natural beauty, cultural richness, and untold stories waiting to be uncovered. From abandoned villages and secluded beaches to picturesque hamlets and cliffside vistas, these hidden treasures offer a glimpse into the island's hidden depths and provide a sense of wonder and discovery for those willing to seek them out. So, as you explore Hvar's hidden gems, may you find moments of magic and beauty that will stay with you long after your journey has ended.

Outdoor odyssey: Exploring Hvar's natural splendours

Embark on an exhilarating journey through Hvar's breath-taking landscapes and diverse terrain, where outdoor enthusiasts will discover a myriad of thrilling activities to satisfy their adventurous spirit. From exploring rugged coastal trails to diving into azure waters teeming with marine life, Hvar offers endless opportunities for outdoor exploration and adventure against the backdrop of its stunning natural beauty.

Hiking and trekking

Lace up your hiking boots and explore Hvar's network of scenic trails that wind through lush forests, ancient olive groves, and rugged coastal cliffs. From leisurely strolls to challenging treks, there are routes suitable for all skill levels, offering panoramic views of the Adriatic Sea and neighbouring islands.

Kayaking and paddleboarding

Experience the thrill of gliding across the crystal-clear waters of the Adriatic Sea on a kayaking or paddleboarding adventure. Explore hidden coves, sea caves, and secluded beaches, or embark on guided tours to discover Hvar's coastal landmarks and marine biodiversity from a unique perspective.

Snorkelling and diving

Dive beneath the surface and discover Hvar's vibrant underwater world, where colourful coral reefs, underwater caves, and an abundance of marine life await. Whether you are a novice snorkeler or a seasoned diver, Hvar's clear waters offer exceptional visibility and countless opportunities for exploration and discovery.

Sailing and boat tours

Set sail on the azure waters surrounding Hvar and embark on a scenic boat tour to explore the island's stunning coastline, hidden bays, and secluded islands. From leisurely cruises aboard traditional wooden boats to adrenaline-pumping speedboat excursions, there are options to suit every taste and budget.

Rock climbing and cliff jumping

Challenge yourself to scale Hvar's rugged cliffs and limestone crags on an exhilarating rock-climbing adventure. With routes suitable for climbers of all levels, as well as opportunities for cliff jumping into the sea, Hvar offers adrenaline-fueled thrills against a backdrop of breath-taking coastal scenery.

Cycling and mountain biking

Explore Hvar's picturesque countryside and charming villages on two wheels with cycling and mountain biking adventures. Follow scenic coastal roads, winding vineyard trails, and rugged mountain paths, taking in panoramic views of the Adriatic Sea and surrounding landscapes along the way.

Windsurfing and kitesurfing

Feel the thrill of riding the wind and waves on a windsurfing or kitesurfing excursion in Hvar's renowned water sports spots. With reliable winds and ideal conditions, Hvar offers excellent opportunities for both beginners and experienced riders to experience the adrenaline rush of these exhilarating sports.

Horseback riding

Discover Hvar's natural beauty from a different perspective with a horseback riding excursion through its scenic countryside. Trot along ancient pathways, through olive groves, and along deserted beaches, immersing yourself in the island's tranquillity and rustic charm as you explore on horseback.

Paragliding and hang gliding

Soar high above Hvar's stunning landscapes and coastline on a paragliding or hang-gliding adventure. Experience the exhilaration of flight as you glide gracefully through the air, taking in bird's-eye views of Hvar's rugged coastline, verdant hillsides, and azure waters below.

Yoga and wellness retreats

Rejuvenate your body, mind, and soul with a yoga and wellness retreat amidst Hvar's serene natural surroundings. Join daily yoga classes, meditation sessions, and holistic wellness activities, immersing yourself in the island's tranquil energy and embracing a healthier, more balanced lifestyle.

As you immerse yourself in Hvar's outdoor playground, you'll discover a world of exhilarating experiences and unforgettable moments that showcase the island's natural beauty and adventurous spirit. Whether you are hiking along scenic trails, exploring underwater wonders, or sailing across the shimmering sea, Hvar's diverse landscape provides the perfect backdrop for outdoor adventure and exploration. So, pack your sense of adventure and get ready to embark on a journey of discovery in one of Croatia's most captivating destinations.

Tradition alive: Immersing in Hvar's festive spirit

Immerse yourself in the rich tapestry of Hvar's local traditions and festivals, where age-old customs blend seamlessly with modern-day celebrations. From centuries-old religious processions to lively wine festivals and colourful carnivals, Hvar offers a diverse array of cultural experiences that capture the essence of island life. Join the locals in honoring ancient rituals, savouring culinary delights, and celebrating the island's vibrant heritage.

Sv. Stjepan (August)

Celebrated on December 26th, this religious festival honours St. Stephen, the patron saint of Hvar. Locals gather in churches for mass, followed by festive processions, traditional music, and dance performances. Enjoy traditional dishes like roasted lamb and fritule, sweet pastries coated in powdered sugar.

Ljeto na Hvaru (June-September)

From June to September, the Hvar Summer Festival showcases a diverse program of cultural events including concerts, theatre performances, art exhibitions, and film screenings. Venues across the town come alive with performances ranging from classical music and opera to contemporary dance and jazz, attracting artists and audiences from around the world.

Ribarske noći u Vrboskoj (July-August)

Held annually in August, this festival celebrates Vrboska's rich fishing heritage with a series of lively events. Enjoy freshly grilled seafood, traditional Dalmatian dishes, and local wines at waterfront taverns. Join in the festivities with live music, folk dances, and boat races, immersing yourself in the vibrant atmosphere of this coastal village.

Hvarski karneval (February/March)

Dating back centuries, the Hvar Carnival is a colourful and lively celebration held in February before the start of Lent. Locals and visitors don elaborate costumes and masks to participate in parades, street performances, and masquerade balls. Experience the carnival's festive spirit with music, dancing, and revelry, as the town comes alive with laughter and merriment.

Festival lavande (June)

Held in June when the island's lavender fields are in full bloom, this festival celebrates Hvar's lavender-growing heritage. Visitors can explore lavender farms, learn about the cultivation process, and purchase handmade lavender products such as oils, soaps, and sachets. Enjoy live music, art exhibits, and culinary delights infused with lavender flavours.

Festival vina Hvar (August)

Held in September during the grape harvest season, this festival showcases Hvar's renowned wine culture. Visitors can taste a variety of local wines, including the famous Plavac Mali red wine and Pošip white wine, while enjoying live music, wine-making demonstrations, and grape-stomping competitions.

Uskršnji mimohod (March/April)

During Holy Week, Hvar's towns and villages host solemn processions to commemorate the Passion of Christ. Locals dressed in traditional attire carry religious statues through the streets, accompanied by chants and prayers. The processions culminate in church services and community gatherings, where Easter traditions are observed with reverence and devotion.

Festival maslinovog ulja (OctoberNovember)

Taking place in November, this festival celebrates Vrboska's olive-growing heritage and the production of extra virgin olive oil. Visitors can learn about olive cultivation and oil pressing techniques, taste freshly pressed olive oil, and sample dishes made with locally sourced olives and olive oil.

Ivanjski krijesovi (June)

Celebrated on the eve of St. John's Day on June 23rd, this ancient tradition involves lighting bonfires along the coast to ward off evil spirits and welcome the summer solstice. Locals gather around the flames to sing, dance, and enjoy traditional dishes such as grilled fish, lamb, and peka.

Whether you are savouring the flavours of local cuisine at a seafood festival, marvelling at the beauty of blooming lavender fields, or dancing in the streets during carnival season, Hvar's traditions and festivals offer unforgettable experiences that resonate with the island's cultural heritage. Through music, food, and community gatherings, these celebrations bring people together, fostering a sense of belonging and camaraderie that embodies the spirit of Hvar.

Hvar hacks: Essential know-how for island travellers

Whether you are drawn to its sun-drenched beaches, historic landmarks, or lively nightlife, Hvar offers a captivating blend of old-world charm and modern sophistication. As you explore this enchanting island destination, here are some travel tips to help you make the most of your experience

Stay hydrated

With its warm climate, it is essential to stay hydrated, especially if you are planning outdoor activities or spending time in the sun. Carry a reusable water bottle and refill it at one of the many public water fountains scattered around the island.

Respect the local customs and culture

Hvar has a rich cultural heritage, so be respectful of local customs and traditions. Dress modestly when visiting religious sites, and be mindful of noise levels, particularly in residential areas during the evening.

Stay sun safe

While enjoying Hvar's beautiful beaches, remember to protect yourself from the sun's rays. Apply sunscreen regularly, wear a hat and sunglasses, and seek shade during the hottest parts of the day to prevent sunburn and heat exhaustion.

Explore off the beaten path

While Hvar's main attractions are undoubtedly stunning, do not be afraid to venture off the beaten path and explore lesser-known areas of the island. You may discover secluded beaches, charming villages, and breath-taking viewpoints that offer a more authentic experience of Hvar.

Be mindful of wildlife

Hvar is home to diverse wildlife, including sea turtles and marine mammals. If you are exploring coastal areas or participating in water activities like snorkelling or diving, remember to observe wildlife from a respectful distance and avoid disturbing their natural habitat.

Respect local customs

While Hvar is known for its vibrant nightlife, it is essential to be mindful of local customs and etiquette. Respect quiet hours, especially in residential areas, and avoid excessive noise late at night to show consideration for local residents.

Support sustainable tourism

Hvar relies heavily on tourism for its economy, so it is essential to support sustainable practices during your visit. Choose eco-friendly accommodations, opt for locally owned businesses and restaurants, and minimize your environmental impact by reducing waste and conserving resources.

Plan ahead for peak season

Hvar can get crowded during the peak tourist season, particularly in July and August. If you are visiting during these months, consider booking accommodations and activities in advance to avoid disappointment and ensure a smooth and enjoyable trip.

Learn basic Croatian phrases

While many locals in Hvar speak English, making an effort to learn a few basic Croatian phrases can go a long way in enhancing your interactions and showing respect for the local culture. Simple greetings like 'Dobro jutro' (Good morning) and 'Hvala' (Thank you) are always appreciated and can help you connect with the friendly locals.

Respect the environment

Hvar's stunning natural landscapes are part of what makes it so special, so be sure to do your part in preserving them for future generations to enjoy. Avoid littering, stay on marked trails when hiking, and refrain from disturbing wildlife. By respecting the environment, you can help ensure that Hvar remains a pristine paradise for years to come.

As you bid farewell to Hvar, take with you fond memories of sun-kissed days, azure waters, and warm hospitality. Whether you are a sun-seeker, a history buff, or a foodie in search of culinary delights, Hvar has undoubtedly left its mark on you. Until next time, may the spirit of Hvar stay with you, inspiring future adventures and unforgettable moments. Safe travels, and do not forget to come back soon!

Island reflections: Capturing memories of Hvar's charms

Hvar, with its storied past and captivating present, is more than just an island—it is a destination that leaves an imprint on the heart. As you bid adieu to its azure waters and sun-soaked beaches, take with you the echoes of ancient tales and the laughter of new friends made along the way. In Hvar's timeless streets and hidden corners, you've uncovered a glimpse of paradise that lingers in your memories long after departure.

With each sunset painting the sky in hues of pink and gold, Hvar whispers a promise of return—a promise to rediscover its secrets, rekindle old adventures, and forge new memories. So, as you sail away from its shores, know that Hvar will always hold a piece of your soul, awaiting your next journey back to its enchanting embrace.

Pucisca: Stonework wonderland

Journey to Pucisca: Coastal craftsmanship and seaside harmony

Nestled on the rugged coastline of the island of Brač, Pucisca stands as a hidden gem awaiting discovery. With its charming white stone buildings cascading down to the shimmering Adriatic Sea, this picturesque town exudes an air of tranquillity and authenticity. As you wander through its narrow streets lined with ancient stone houses and fragrant citrus trees, you'll find yourself transported to a bygone era where time seems to stand still.

Pucisca's beauty lies not only in its stunning natural surroundings but also in the warmth of its people and the rich tapestry of its history and culture. Known for its centuries-old tradition of stone masonry, the town boasts exquisite architectural marvels crafted from the island's famed white limestone. From the majestic bell tower of the Parish Church of St. Jerome to the elegant facades of its historic buildings, Pucisca invites visitors to immerse themselves in its timeless charm and experience the allure of island life at its finest.

Crafted in time: Pucisca's stone heritage on display

Pucisca, with its rich historical heritage, holds a prominent place in the annals of Dalmatia's history. Dating back to antiquity, the town's roots can be traced to the Illyrians and Romans who once inhabited the region. However, it was during the Venetian era in the 15th century that Pucisca flourished, becoming renowned for its skilled stone masons and the exceptional quality of its white limestone. The town's stone-carving tradition reached its zenith during this period, shaping its identity and leaving an indelible mark on its architecture.

One of the most significant landmarks of Pucisca's historical significance is the School of Stonemasonry, founded in the 17th century. This esteemed institution continues to impart the ancient craft of stone carving to aspiring artisans, preserving a tradition that has been passed down through generations. The town's streets are adorned with exquisite examples of stonework, from intricate sculptures to elaborate facades, each bearing witness to Pucisca's enduring legacy as a centre of stone masonry excellence.

Tradition alive: Pucisca's coastal crafts and culture

Pucisca's local culture is deeply intertwined with its rich heritage of stone masonry, a craft that has shaped the identity and livelihoods of its residents for centuries. As you wander through the town's narrow cobblestone streets, you'll encounter workshops and studios where skilled artisans continue to carve and sculpt the island's famed white limestone, keeping alive a tradition that dates back to ancient times. This craftsmanship is not merely a profession but a way of life, passed down from generation to generation, and celebrated as an integral part of Pucisca's cultural fabric.

In addition to its renowned stone masonry, Pucisca is also home to a vibrant community that takes pride in its traditions and customs. Throughout the year, the town comes alive with festivals, music, and dance, offering visitors a glimpse into the rhythms of island life. From the lively summer celebrations of St. Stephen's Day to the solemn processions of Holy Week, Pucisca's calendar is filled with events that honour its heritage and bring people together in joyous camaraderie. Whether you are sampling local delicacies at a traditional taverna or joining in the festivities of a local fiesta, you'll find that the warmth and hospitality of Pucisca's residents are as enduring as the stone that shapes their town.

Limestone wonders: Pucisca's coastal landmarks

Step into the enchanting town of Pucisca, where history whispers through the cobblestone streets and the Adriatic breeze carries the scent of salt and pine. Here, amidst the rugged beauty of Brac Island, lies a destination that transcends time, inviting travellers to immerse themselves in its rich tapestry of culture and tradition. From ancient stone quarries to bustling markets brimming with local delicacies, Pucisca is a treasure trove waiting to be discovered.

Pucisca stone masonry school

Nestled within the town's historic streets, the Stone Masonry School is a testament to Pucisca's rich heritage of stonemasonry. Founded in 1909, the school has played a vital role in preserving and promoting this traditional craft. Visitors can observe skilled artisans at work, shaping the famous Brac limestone into exquisite sculptures, architectural elements, and artworks.

Pucisca cultural centre

Housed in a beautifully restored building overlooking the harbour, the Cultural Centre is a hub of creativity and community spirit. Here, locals and visitors alike can immerse themselves in Pucisca's vibrant cultural scene through a diverse range of exhibitions, workshops, and performances. From art shows and music concerts to theatre productions and film screenings, the centre offers something for everyone to enjoy.

Dragons' cave

Tucked away in the rugged landscape surrounding Pucisca, Dragons' Cave is a natural wonder steeped in myth and legend. As you venture into its depths, you'll be greeted by a mesmerizing display of stalactites and stalagmites, illuminated by shafts of sunlight filtering through the cave's entrance. According to local lore, this mystical cavern was once the domain of dragons, adding an air of enchantment to your exploration.

Pucisca promenade

This charming waterfront promenade invites visitors to take a leisurely stroll along the azure waters of the Adriatic Sea. Lined with palm trees and offering panoramic views of the coastline, the promenade is the perfect spot to unwind and soak in the coastal ambiance. Along the way, you'll find quaint cafes and ice cream parlours where you can savour delicious treats while watching the boats sail by.

Pucisca olive oil museum

Delve into the rich history and heritage of olive oil production in Pucisca at the Olive Oil Museum. Housed in a historic stone building, the museum showcases the traditional methods of olive oil extraction used by generations of local farmers. Visitors can learn about the cultivation of olive trees, the harvesting process, and the art of pressing olives to produce high-quality olive oil. Interactive exhibits and guided tours offer a fascinating insight into this essential aspect of Pucisca's agricultural heritage.

St. Jerome's church

Standing majestically atop a hill overlooking the town, St. Jerome's Church is a magnificent example of Baroque architecture. Its elegant facade is adorned with intricate carvings and statues, drawing the eye of passers-by. Inside, the church boasts a serene atmosphere, with beautiful marble altars, ornate frescoes, and delicate stained-glass windows creating an aura of tranquillity.

Church of St. Stephen

Dating back to the 18th century, the Church of St. Stephen is a prominent landmark in Pucisca's skyline. Its distinctive bell tower rises gracefully above the town, providing a striking focal point against the backdrop of the Adriatic Sea. Step inside the church to admire its Baroque architecture and ornate interior, which includes exquisite altarpieces, intricate woodcarvings, and captivating religious artwork.

Pucisca beaches

Pucisca boasts several pristine beaches that offer idyllic settings for sunbathing, swimming, and water sports. From secluded coves with crystal-clear waters to lively beaches with beach bars and water sports facilities, there is a spot to suit every preference. Spend lazy days basking in the Mediterranean sunshine, exploring hidden bays accessible only by boat, or snorkelling among colourful marine life in the tranquil waters of the Adriatic.

Pucisca sculpture park

Tucked away in a scenic spot overlooking the town, the Pucisca Sculpture Park is a unique outdoor gallery showcasing the works of local and international artists. Wander through the park's lush gardens and discover a diverse collection of sculptures crafted from various materials, including stone, wood, and metal.

Pucisca maritime museum

Dive into the seafaring history of Pucisca at the Maritime Museum, housed in a historic stone building overlooking the harbour. Through engaging exhibits and artifacts, the museum traces the town's maritime heritage, from its shipbuilding traditions to its connections with trade and navigation. Visitors can explore model ships, navigational instruments, and learn about the lives of sailors and fishermen who once sailed the waters of the Adriatic.

Pucisca harbour

The vibrant heart of Pucisca, this picturesque harbour is a delightful blend of tradition and charm. Lined with colourful fishing boats bobbing gently on the crystal-clear waters, the harbour offers a mesmerizing view of the Adriatic Sea. Visitors can take leisurely strolls along the waterfront promenade, pausing to admire the quaint stone houses and enjoy the fresh sea breeze.

As you bid farewell to Pucisca, take with you the memories of its serene harbour, centuries-old churches, and warm hospitality. Whether you spent your days admiring the stone masonry craftsmanship or soaking in the tranquil beauty of Dragons' Cave, Pucisca has undoubtedly left its mark on your soul. As you continue your journey, may the spirit of Pucisca stay with you, inspiring new adventures and unforgettable experiences. Until we meet again, farewell, and may your travels be filled with joy and discovery.

Savouring stone and sea: Pucisca's culinary harmony

Embark on a culinary journey through the charming town of Pucisca, where the flavours of the Adriatic come to life in a symphony of taste and tradition. Nestled along the shores of Brac Island, Pucisca boasts a vibrant culinary scene that celebrates the region's rich heritage and bounty of fresh ingredients. From savoury seafood delicacies to hearty island fare, each dish tells a story of the land and sea, inviting visitors to savour the essence of Dalmatia.

Brac lamb

Pucisca's renowned Brac lamb is a culinary masterpiece, celebrated for its tenderness and rich flavour. Raised on the island's pristine pastures, the lamb is slow-roasted to perfection, allowing the meat to become incredibly tender while retaining its natural juices. Seasoned with aromatic herbs like rosemary, thyme, and oregano, each bite is a symphony of Mediterranean flavours that reflect the island's bountiful landscape.

Hrapocusa cake

Hrapocusa, a traditional Dalmatian dessert, holds a special place in the hearts of Pucisca locals. Crafted from a blend of ground almonds, sweet honey, and fragrant citrus zest, this moist and aromatic cake is a delightful treat for any occasion. With a dense yet fluffy texture and a delicate sweetness, Hrapocusa embodies the essence of Dalmatian cuisine and is often enjoyed with a cup of strong Croatian coffee.

Zlatan Otok wine

Zlatan Otok wine is the pride of Pucisca, a testament to the island's rich winemaking tradition. Crafted from indigenous grape varieties such as Plavac Mali and Posip, Zlatan Otok wines capture the essence of Brac's terroir with their bold flavours and complex aromas. From crisp and refreshing whites to full-bodied reds, each bottle tells a story of the island's maritime climate and limestone-rich soil, making it the perfect accompaniment to any meal or celebration in Pucisca.

Seafood risotto

Pucisca's seafood risotto is a culinary treasure that showcases the freshest catch from the Adriatic Sea. Made with locally sourced mussels, clams, shrimp, and squid, this creamy rice dish is infused with the flavours of the sea and seasoned with fragrant herbs like saffron, parsley, and bay leaf.

Anchovies in olive oil

Anchovies in olive oil are a beloved delicacy in Pucisca, prized for their intense umami flavour and silky texture. Caught in the pristine waters of the Adriatic Sea, these small fish are carefully preserved in locally produced olive oil, allowing them to develop a rich, savoury taste that pairs perfectly with crusty bread and a glass of wine.

Almond rakija

Almond rakija is a traditional Croatian fruit brandy that is particularly popular in Pucisca. Made from locally grown almonds, this smooth and aromatic spirit is distilled to perfection, resulting in a rich and flavourful liquor with hints of almond blossom and warm spices. Sipped neat or used as a base for cocktails, almond rakija is a delightful way to end a meal and toast to the beauty of Brac Island.

Prosciutto and cheese plate

Pucisca's prosciutto and cheese plate showcases the region's rich culinary heritage and artisanal craftsmanship. Thinly sliced Dalmatian prosciutto, aged to perfection and bursting with flavour, is paired with an array of locally produced cheeses, including sheep's milk cheese and Pag cheese. Served with freshly baked bread, homemade olive tapenade, and a drizzle of honey, this simple yet elegant dish is a true delight for the senses.

Almond cake

Almond cake, or mandulat, is a beloved dessert in Pucisca that showcases the island's rich culinary heritage. Made with locally grown almonds, which are ground into a fine flour, the cake is moist, dense, and bursting with nutty flavour. Traditionally served with a dollop of whipped cream or a drizzle of honey, almond cake is a simple yet irresistible treat that pairs perfectly with a cup of strong Croatian coffee.

Stuffed squid

Stuffed squid is a popular dish in Pucisca that highlights the bounty of the Adriatic Sea. Fresh squid is cleaned and stuffed with a savoury mixture of breadcrumbs, garlic, parsley, and local spices before being grilled to perfection. The squid becomes tender and juicy, while the filling infuses it with irresistible flavours.

Truffle risotto

Truffles are a prized culinary treasure, and in Pucisca, they are used to elevate classic dishes such as risotto to new heights. Truffle risotto is a luxurious and indulgent dish that showcases the earthy flavours of these prized fungi. Arborio rice is cooked slowly in a rich broth infused with truffle oil, then finished with generous shavings of fresh truffles for an unforgettable dining experience.

Fig tart

Pucisca's fig tart is a delectable dessert that celebrates the island's abundance of fresh figs. The tart's buttery crust provides the perfect base for a luscious filling made from ripe figs, honey, and a hint of citrus zest. Baked to golden perfection, each slice of fig tart is a delightful balance of sweet and tart flavours, reminiscent of lazy summer afternoons spent under the Mediterranean sun.

Exploring the culinary delights of Pucisca offers a journey through the rich flavours and traditions of Dalmatian cuisine. From fresh seafood dishes like black risotto and stuffed squid to gourmet delights such as truffle risotto and almond cake, each culinary experience is a testament to the region's vibrant culinary heritage. Whether savouring a leisurely meal overlooking the azure waters of the Adriatic Sea or sampling street food at a local market, every bite tells a story of the island's bounty and the passion of its people for good food and company. As the sun sets on another day in Pucisca, the memories of these culinary adventures linger, leaving a lasting impression of the gastronomic wonders of this charming Dalmatian town.

Unearthing Pucisca's coastal secrets: Hidden gems await

Pučišća, a picturesque town on the island of Brač, is a treasure trove of hidden gems waiting to be discovered. From secluded beaches and hidden coves to historic landmarks and local artisans, Pučišća offers a unique blend of history, culture, and natural beauty that is sure to captivate visitors. Here are some of the town's hidden gems that you won't want to miss.

Stonemason workshop

Immerse yourself in the world of Brač stone at the stonemason workshops, where skilled artisans transform the island's famous white stone into intricate sculptures, ornaments, and architectural elements. These hidden gems offer a unique opportunity to witness the craftsmanship and techniques that have shaped Pučišća's identity for centuries.

Kopacina cave

Located on the outskirts of Pučišća, this prehistoric cave dates back to the Neolithic period, offering a glimpse into the town's distant past. Kopačina Cave features ancient carvings, remnants of prehistoric life, and a fascinating geological history. Visitors can take guided tours of the cave, learn about its significance, and marvel at the natural beauty of its chambers and rock formations.

Vela Spila cave

Delve into the depths of history at Vela Spila Cave, an archaeological marvel that offers a glimpse into Pucisca's ancient past. Venture into the darkness of its cavernous chambers, where the echoes of bygone eras linger in the air. Here, amidst stalactites and stalagmites that have stood the test of time, archaeologists have uncovered a treasure trove of artifacts dating back to the Neolithic period. Marvel at the skill of our ancestors as you behold primitive tools, ceremonial objects, and intricate carvings that offer tantalizing clues about early human life on Brač Island.

Lozisca village

Discover the picturesque charm of Ložišća Village, a hidden gem nestled amidst the rugged landscapes of Brač Island. Wander through its narrow cobblestone streets, flanked by stone houses adorned with vibrant bougainvillea and fragrant citrus trees. Immerse yourself in the timeless rhythm of local life as you encounter friendly faces and warm smiles at every turn.

Lucice bay

Tucked away along the rugged coastline, Lučice Bay beckons with its pristine waters and tranquil ambiance. Surrounded by pine forests and olive groves, this hidden gem is a sanctuary for those seeking a peaceful retreat. The pebble beach and crystal-clear sea create a perfect setting for relaxation, swimming, and snorkelling, offering a slice of paradise away from the crowds.

Duboka bay

Indulge in the ultimate island getaway at Duboka Bay, a hidden oasis of serenity and natural beauty nestled along the rugged coastline of Brač Island. Escape the crowds and discover your own private slice of paradise on its secluded shores, where crystal-clear waters lap gently against sun-drenched cliffs. Dive into the azure depths and explore vibrant underwater worlds teeming with marine life, or simply bask in the sun's warm embrace as you soak up the breath-taking coastal scenery.

Dolina Blaca monastery

Embark on a pilgrimage to Dolina Blaca Monastery, a hidden sanctuary nestled amidst the rugged landscapes of Brač Island. Journey along winding paths that wind through pine-scented forests and rocky ravines, leading to this remote and awe-inspiring spiritual retreat. Founded in the 16th century by Glagolitic priests seeking refuge from the Ottoman invasion, the monastery stands as a testament to faith, resilience, and the enduring spirit of human endeavour. Explore its ancient chapels, libraries, and living quarters, marvelling at the intricate frescoes and artifacts that adorn its hallowed halls.

Vidova Gora

Ascend the slopes of Vidova Gora, the crown jewel of Brač Island, and be rewarded with sweeping vistas that stretch as far as the eye can see. Wander through pine-scented forests, tracing paths once trodden by ancient civilizations, and feel the exhilaration as you reach the summit. From this vantage point, the Adriatic unfolds like a masterpiece, its azure hues blending seamlessly with the sky, while distant islands punctuate the horizon.

Pucisca reveals itself as a hidden gem waiting to be discovered, offering a tapestry of natural wonders, cultural treasures, and serene escapes for the intrepid traveller. From the mystical depths of Kopačina Cave to the tranquil shores of Duboka Bay, each hidden gem beckons with its own unique allure, inviting visitors to immerse themselves in the timeless beauty of Brač Island. Whether exploring ancient monasteries, wandering through picturesque villages, or delving into the rich history of olive oil production, Pucisca promises an unforgettable journey filled with moments of wonder and reflection.

Embracing nature: Outdoor pursuits in Pucisca's realm

Nestled on the rugged shores of Brač Island, Pucisca offers a playground for outdoor enthusiasts seeking adventure amidst stunning natural beauty. From rugged coastal cliffs to lush inland landscapes, this charming town provides a plethora of outdoor activities to satisfy every adventurer's craving for excitement and exploration.

Hiking and trekking

Embark on scenic hiking trails that wind through Pucisca's pristine countryside, offering breath-taking views of the Adriatic Sea and surrounding islands. Explore the island's diverse terrain, from rugged coastal paths to verdant forests, and discover hidden gems along the way, including ancient ruins and secluded beaches.

Cycling tours

Pedal your way through picturesque villages and rolling hills on a cycling tour of Brač Island. Explore charming hamlets, olive groves, and vineyards as you navigate scenic routes that showcase the island's rich cultural heritage and stunning landscapes.

Water sports

Take to the crystal-clear waters of the Adriatic Sea and indulge in an array of water sports activities, including kayaking, paddleboarding, and snorkelling. Explore hidden coves, sea caves, and underwater marine life as you glide across the azure waters, soaking in the sun-drenched beauty of Brač's coastline.

Sailing excursions

Set sail on the shimmering Adriatic waters and embark on a sailing excursion to explore the hidden coves, secluded beaches, and charming coastal villages surrounding Pucisca. Feel the sea breeze in your hair as you navigate Brač Island's pristine coastline aboard a traditional wooden sailing boat or a modern yacht, with options for private charters or group tours.

Scenic drives

Discover the beauty of Brač Island's diverse landscapes with a scenic drive through Pucisca's countryside, dotted with olive groves, vineyards, and ancient stone villages. Follow winding coastal roads that offer panoramic views of the Adriatic Sea and neighbouring islands, stopping along the way to capture stunning vistas and explore hidden gems off the beaten path.

Nature walks and birdwatching

Explore Pucisca's natural wonders on leisurely nature walks through lush forests and along coastal paths, where you can encounter native flora and fauna, including aromatic herbs, wildflowers, and migratory birds. Bring your binoculars and birdwatching guide to spot a variety of avian species nesting in the island's diverse habitats, from woodlands to wetlands.

Yoga and wellness retreats

Indulge in a rejuvenating yoga and wellness retreat in Pucisca, where you can find inner peace and harmony amidst the island's tranquil surroundings. Join daily yoga sessions led by experienced instructors, practice meditation on secluded beaches, and nourish your body with wholesome Mediterranean cuisine, all while immersing yourself in the island's natural beauty.

Mountain biking adventures

Hop on a mountain bike and explore Pucisca's rugged terrain and scenic trails, offering adrenaline-pumping rides and breath-taking views of the Adriatic coastline. Navigate through pine forests, rocky paths, and ancient olive groves as you discover hidden gems and panoramic viewpoints, making each biking excursion an unforgettable adventure.

Rock climbing excursions
Challenge your limits and scale the towering cliffs and limestone formations that surround Pucisca, where experienced guides lead rock climbing excursions suitable for climbers of all levels.

Sea kayaking tours

Paddle along the crystal-clear waters of the Adriatic Sea on a sea kayaking tour, exploring hidden coves, sea caves, and remote beaches inaccessible by land. Glide past rugged coastline and underwater rock formations, pausing to snorkel and swim in secluded bays, where you can observe colourful marine life and immerse yourself in the serenity of nature.

Horseback riding escapes

Embark on a horseback riding adventure through Pucisca's picturesque countryside and along the scenic coastline of Brač Island, where experienced equestrian guides lead trail rides for riders of all skill levels. Explore hidden paths, olive groves, and vineyards on horseback, enjoying the tranquillity and beauty of the island's natural landscapes.

As the sun sets on your outdoor adventures in Pucisca, take a moment to reflect on the beauty and serenity of Brač Island's natural landscapes. Whether hiking along rugged coastal trails, cycling through picturesque villages, or exploring the underwater world of the Adriatic, Pucisca offers endless opportunities for outdoor exploration and discovery. As you bid farewell to this enchanting town, may the memories of your outdoor escapades linger, inspiring future adventures in Croatia's stunning island paradise.

Celebrating coastal heritage: Pucisca's vibrant festive scene

Throughout the year, Pucisca hosts a variety of festivals and events that showcase the island's unique identity and bring together residents and visitors alike in celebration. From religious feasts to film screenings, olive harvests to music evenings, each festival offers a glimpse into the heart and soul of this picturesque Dalmatian community.

Festival Sv. Križa (May)

The Festival of the Holy Cross, celebrated on May 3rd, is a significant religious event honoring the patron saint of Pucisca, Saint Cross. This festive occasion features colourful processions, solemn church services, and vibrant cultural performances, including traditional folk music and dance. Locals and visitors alike gather to pay their respects and participate in the joyful atmosphere, enjoying traditional delicacies and local wines.

Bracki Filmski Festival (August)

The Brac Film Festival, held annually in July, is a cinematic extravaganza that attracts filmmakers, artists, and film enthusiasts from around the world. This dynamic event showcases a diverse selection of international and Croatian independent films, documentaries, and shorts. Attendees have the opportunity to engage in screenings, discussions, and workshops, fostering dialogue and appreciation for the art of filmmaking.

Ljetni Muzički Večeri (July-August)

Pucisca comes alive with melodious tunes during the Summer Music Evenings held throughout the summer months. This musical extravaganza showcases a diverse array of performances, ranging from classical concerts and folk ensembles to jazz bands and contemporary acts.

Seljačke svečanosti (August)

Experience the rustic charm of Brač's countryside during the Village Festivities, where local communities gather to celebrate their heritage and traditions. Visitors can partake in folkloric dances, traditional crafts demonstrations, and authentic gastronomic experiences featuring locally sourced ingredients.

Festival maslinarstva (October)

Celebrated in October, the Olive Harvest Festival pays homage to Pucisca's longstanding tradition of olive cultivation and production. Visitors can immerse themselves in the olive-picking process, participate in olive oil tastings, and learn about traditional harvesting techniques. The festival also features cultural performances, artisanal markets offering local products, and culinary delights highlighting the versatility of olive oil in Dalmatian cuisine.

Ljetni karneval (August)

The Summer Carnival, held annually in July, is a lively event that transforms the streets of Pucisca into a vibrant carnival procession. Colourful floats, extravagant costumes, and festive music create an atmosphere of revelry and merriment. Visitors can join in the parade or watch from the side-lines as dancers, jugglers, and performers entertain the crowds.

Festival bračkih ovaca (April)

The Festival of Brač Island Sheep, typically held in September, honours the vital role of sheep farming in the region's cultural heritage. Visitors can witness traditional sheep-shearing demonstrations, sample artisanal sheep cheese, and learn about the time-honoured practices of wool production. The festival also features exhibitions on sheep breeding, folk music performances, and competitions showcasing local craftsmanship.

Dan sv. Jeronima (September)

The Day of St. Jerome, observed on September 30th, is a special occasion dedicated to the patron saint of Pucisca. Religious processions, solemn Mass services, and cultural performances pay homage to St. Jerome's legacy and significance in the community. The day is also marked by communal gatherings, where locals share traditional dishes and engage in heartfelt conversations, fostering a sense of unity and reverence.

Međunarodni simpozij kamenih skulptura (July)

The International Stone Sculpture Symposium, held biennially, showcases the artistic talent and craftsmanship of sculptors from around the world. During the symposium, artists gather in Pucisca to create monumental stone sculptures inspired by the town's rich cultural heritage and natural surroundings. Visitors can observe the creative process first-hand and marvel at the breath-taking sculptures that adorn public spaces, parks, and promenades throughout the town.

As you experience the colourful tapestry of local traditions and festivals in Pucisca, may you be enchanted by the spirit of camaraderie and cultural pride that permeates each celebration. Whether you are joining in the jubilant processions of the Festival of the Holy Cross or savouring the flavours of the Olive Harvest Festival, may these experiences create lasting memories and deepen your connection to the rich heritage of Brač Island. As you bid farewell to Pucisca, may the vibrant energy of its festivals stay with you, inspiring a return journey to partake in future festivities and immerse yourself once again in the warmth of Dalmatian hospitality.

Pucisca uncovered: Insider advice for coastal travellers

Pučišća, a hidden gem on the island of Brač, offers a unique blend of history, culture, and natural beauty waiting to be explored. For travellers seeking an authentic Dalmatian experience, Pučišća's charm lies in its stonemasonry heritage, pristine beaches, and warm hospitality. Here are some travel tips to make the most of your visit to this picturesque town.

Accommodation

Secure your stay in advance, especially during the bustling summer season, to ensure availability. Options range from charming family-run guesthouses to elegant boutique hotels, each offering a unique glimpse into the local way of life against the stunning backdrop of the Adriatic Sea.

Explore the town on foot

Pucisca is a compact and picturesque town that is best explored on foot. Wander through its charming streets, admire the traditional stone houses, and discover hidden gems around every corner. Do not forget to wear comfortable walking shoes and carry a map to navigate the narrow alleyways.

Embrace the Island lifestyle

Pucisca embodies the laid-back island lifestyle of Brač, so take the time to slow down and soak in the relaxed atmosphere. Spend lazy days lounging on pristine beaches, swimming in crystal-clear waters, and savouring breath-taking sunsets.

Respect local customs and traditions

As a visitor to Pucisca, it is important to respect the local customs and traditions of the community. Dress modestly when visiting religious sites, observe quiet hours in residential areas, and follow any cultural norms or etiquette practices. By showing consideration for the local way of life, you'll enhance your travel experience and leave a positive impression on the residents.

Getting around

Rent a scooter or bicycle to explore Pucisca and its surroundings independently. This allows you to navigate narrow streets and discover secluded beaches unreachable by car. Alternatively, hire a local guide for an immersive experience, gaining insights into the town's history and culture while uncovering hidden gems off the beaten path.

Navigating narrow streets

Given the town's charming but narrow streets, it is advisable to explore on foot or by bicycle. This allows you to fully appreciate its beauty and also find hidden spots that are inaccessible by car.

Exploring nearby attractions

While in Pucisca, consider taking day trips to explore nearby attractions such as the Vidova Gora mountain, the highest peak on the island of Brač, offering breath-taking panoramic views of the Adriatic Sea. You can also visit other charming towns on the island, such as Supetar and Bol.

Shopping for local souvenirs

Take a stroll through Pucisca's artisan shops and boutiques, where you can find unique souvenirs and gifts crafted by local artists. Whether it is handmade ceramics, jewelry, or textiles, you are sure to find something special to remind you of your time in this enchanting town.

Enjoying water activities

Take advantage of Pucisca's coastal location by participating in various water activities. Whether it is swimming, snorkelling, kayaking, or sailing, there are plenty of opportunities to enjoy the crystal-clear waters of the Adriatic Sea and soak up the Mediterranean sunshine.

Learning basic Croatian phrases

While many locals in Pucisca may speak English, knowing a few basic Croatian phrases can enhance your travel experience and show respect for the local culture. Practice common greetings, expressions of gratitude, and simple phrases for ordering food or asking for directions.

With its captivating blend of history, craftsmanship, and natural beauty, Pucisca offers a memorable travel experience for those seeking an off-the-beaten-path destination in Croatia. By exploring the town's stonemasonry heritage, historic sites, and culinary delights, visitors can immerse themselves in the authentic charm of Pučišća and create lasting memories of their Dalmatian adventure.

Reflecting on Pucisca: Coastal magic lingers in stonework symphony

As twilight descends upon Pucisca, the town's timeless beauty reveals itself in a symphony of colours and whispers of history. Each cobblestone street and weathered façade tells a story of craftsmanship and resilience, a testament to the enduring spirit of its people. In the quiet moments before nightfall, Pucisca invites reflection—a chance to ponder the intricacies of its stone-carving tradition and the generations of artisans who have shaped its identity.

As you bid farewell to Pucisca, carry with you the memories of its sun-drenched days and starlit nights, a treasure trove of moments that will forever be etched in your heart. Whether it is the gentle lapping of waves against the harbour walls or the laughter of locals echoing through the streets, Pucisca leaves an imprint on your soul, a reminder of the beauty and resilience found in the simplest of moments. Until we meet again, may the spirit of Pucisca guide your journey, and may its timeless charm continue to inspire wonder wherever your travels may lead.

Labin: Coastal gem of Istria

Discover Labin: Istrian charms by the Adriatic shore

Perched atop the Istrian peninsula, overlooking the azure waters of the Adriatic Sea, Labin beckons travellers with its enchanting blend of history, culture, and natural beauty. As you meander through the cobbled streets of its ancient Old Town, you'll be transported back in time to an era of medieval splendour and Renaissance elegance. From the imposing walls of the Fortica to the charming squares adorned with centuries-old churches and palaces, Labin's rich architectural heritage reflects its storied past as a bustling mining and trading hub.

But Labin is more than just a picturesque backdrop for history buffs; it is a vibrant destination where tradition meets modernity in perfect harmony. With its bustling markets, quaint cafes, and lively cultural events, the town pulsates with the rhythm of everyday life. Whether you are exploring the winding alleyways of the Old Town or soaking up the sun on the nearby beaches, Labin invites you to embark on a journey of discovery and immerse yourself in its timeless allure.

Labin's timeless treasures: Icons of the ages

Labin, steeped in history and heritage, boasts a remarkable legacy that spans millennia. Its origins trace back to the time of the Illyrians, who first settled in the region, followed by the Romans who established a thriving community known as Albona. Over the centuries, Labin evolved into a fortified medieval town, its strategic hilltop location making it a coveted stronghold for various rulers, including the Venetians and the Austro-Hungarian Empire. This tumultuous past is evident in the town's architectural marvels, from the imposing Labin Fort to the well-preserved medieval streets adorned with centuries-old facades.

One of Labin's most significant chapters in history is its role as a centre of coal mining during the industrial revolution. In the 19th and early 20th centuries, Labin's mines were a vital source of coal for the region, driving economic growth and shaping the town's development. The legacy of this industrial era is still visible today, with remnants of mining infrastructure dotting the landscape and serving as a reminder of Labin's industrial past. Through the centuries, Labin has endured wars, revolutions, and social upheavals, yet its resilient spirit and rich heritage continue to fascinate and inspire visitors from near and far.

Celebrating community: Labin's rich cultural heritage

Labin's vibrant local culture is a testament to the town's diverse heritage and the resilience of its people. Rooted in centuries-old traditions and influenced by various civilizations that have left their mark on the region, Labin's cultural tapestry is as rich and varied as its storied history. From the vibrant folk festivals that celebrate Istrian music and dance to the centuries-old customs that honour the town's patron saints, Labin offers visitors a glimpse into the authentic rhythms of life in Istria.

The town's cultural scene is further enriched by its thriving arts community, with galleries and studios showcasing the work of local painters, sculptors, and craftsmen. Visitors can explore Labin's artistic heritage at the Labin Art Republic, a vibrant cultural centre housed in a renovated 19th-century villa. Here, exhibitions, workshops, and performances provide insight into the creative spirit that thrives amidst Labin's picturesque surroundings. As you wander through the town's streets, you'll encounter quaint artisan shops and cozy cafes where locals gather to share stories, preserving the traditions and camaraderie that define Labin's unique cultural identity.

Storied sites: Discovering Labin's coastal icons

With its rich history, stunning architecture, and scenic landscapes, Labin offers a treasure trove of landmarks and points of interest waiting to be discovered. From exploring the cobblestone streets of the Old Town to admiring panoramic views from the fortress, there is something to captivate every visitor in this charming Croatian destination.

Labin art gallery

Housed in the Palace Battiala-Lazzarini, the Labin Art Gallery is a cultural hub showcasing the works of renowned Croatian artists alongside contemporary exhibitions. The gallery's permanent collection features diverse art forms, including paintings, sculptures, and ceramics, offering insight into Istria's rich artistic heritage.

Fortress of Labin

Dominating the skyline of Labin, the Fortress of Labin is a symbol of the town's medieval past and strategic importance. Built in the 11th century to defend against invaders, the fortress offers a fascinating journey through history. Explore its ancient ramparts, defensive towers, and underground tunnels, where interactive exhibits and archaeological finds reveal the tumultuous events that shaped the region. The fortress also hosts cultural events and concerts, adding to its allure as a must-visit landmark.

Glowing rocks beach

Experience the enchanting phenomenon of Glowing Rocks Beach, where the coastline comes alive with bioluminescent plankton after nightfall. The mesmerizing blue glow emanating from the water creates a magical ambiance, perfect for a romantic evening stroll or a unique midnight swim.

Sveta marina bay

Nestled along the rugged coastline, Sveta Marina Bay offers a tranquil retreat for those seeking solitude and natural beauty. Surrounded by lush greenery and crystal-clear waters, this hidden gem is ideal for swimming, snorkelling, and sunbathing. Explore the secluded coves and rocky cliffs, where you can soak in the panoramic views of the Adriatic Sea and enjoy the serenity of your surroundings.

Old town of Labin

Nestled atop a limestone hill, Labin's Old Town is a picturesque maze of narrow cobblestone streets and historic buildings. Dating back to the Middle Ages, it boasts well-preserved architecture, charming squares, and artisan shops. Wander through its medieval alleys to discover hidden gems like the Town Museum and the Gothic Church of St. Stephen.

Truffle hunting excursions

Delve into the world of gastronomic delights with truffle hunting excursions in the lush forests surrounding Labin. Accompanied by experienced truffle hunters and their trained dogs, you'll embark on a thrilling adventure in search of the elusive Istrian truffle. Learn about the secrets of truffle hunting and the importance of these prized fungi in Istrian cuisine. After the hunt, indulge in a delectable truffle-themed meal featuring freshly harvested truffles paired with local specialties, offering a true taste of Istria's culinary heritage.

St. Florian's church

Discover the architectural marvel of St. Florian's Church, a stunning example of Baroque-style design located in the heart of Labin. Admire the intricate details of its façade, adorned with ornate sculptures and elegant stonework, as you step inside this sacred sanctuary. Marvel at the majestic altarpiece and exquisite frescoes that adorn the interior, depicting scenes from the life of St. Florian and other religious motifs.

The Palace Negri-Dobrila

Explore the grandeur of the Palace Negri-Dobrila, an elegant Renaissance-style mansion that stands as a testament to Labin's rich history and cultural heritage. Originally built in the 17th century by the influential Negri family, the palace boasts exquisite architectural details and opulent interiors that reflect the wealth and status of its former owners. Admire the intricate stone carvings, graceful archways, and majestic courtyard as you wander through its halls, and learn about the palace's storied past through informative exhibits and guided tours.

Bartul Kasic square

Experience the vibrant energy of Bartul Kašić Square, the bustling heart of Labin's social and cultural scene. Named after the renowned Croatian linguist and lexicographer, the square serves as a lively gathering place for locals and visitors alike. Situated amidst historic buildings and charming cafes, the square is a hub of activity, hosting festivals, concerts, and cultural events throughout the year.

Church of St. Stephen

The Church of St. Stephen stands as a testament to Labin's spiritual heritage and architectural prowess. Dating back to the 15th century, this Gothic masterpiece boasts a stunning facade adorned with intricate stone carvings and a towering bell tower. Step inside to admire its richly decorated interior, featuring Baroque altars, ornate frescoes, and precious religious artifacts.

As you bid farewell to Labin, take with you the memories of its storied past and vibrant culture. Whether you've explored its historic sites, immersed yourself in its art scene, or simply enjoyed its scenic beauty, Labin has undoubtedly left an indelible mark on your journey. As you continue your travels, carry with you the spirit of discovery and the desire to explore more of Croatia's hidden gems.

A Culinary voyage: Labin's fusion of flavours

Labin offers a culinary experience that reflects the region's diverse culinary traditions and influences. From hearty Istrian stews to fresh seafood delicacies, the local cuisine of Labin is sure to tantalize your taste buds and leave you craving for more. Join us on a gastronomic journey through the streets of Labin as we explore its hidden culinary gems and savour the flavours of Istria.

Istrian prosciutto

Labin is renowned for its exquisite Istrian prosciutto, a cured ham delicacy that embodies the essence of Istrian cuisine. Made from locally raised pigs and seasoned with sea salt and aromatic herbs, Istrian prosciutto is air-dried for months to develop its distinctive flavour and tender texture.

Truffles

Delight your senses with the earthy aroma and intense flavour of Istrian truffles, often referred to as 'black diamonds'. Labin's surrounding forests are abundant with these prized fungi, which are prized for their culinary versatility and luxurious taste. Indulge in truffle-infused dishes such as creamy risottos, handmade pasta, and savoury sauces, showcasing the rich and distinctive flavours of Istria.

Manestra

Warm your soul with a hearty bowl of Istrian manestra, a traditional bean soup beloved by locals and visitors alike. Made with locally sourced beans, vegetables, and cured meats, manestra is slow-cooked to perfection, allowing the flavours to meld together beautifully. Served piping hot with a drizzle of extra virgin olive oil and crusty bread, manestra is the ultimate comfort food that captures the heart and soul of Istrian cuisine.

Istrian pasta

Indulge in the comfort of Istrian pasta, known as fuži, which are handmade pasta twists that capture the essence of traditional Istrian cuisine. Served with a variety of sauces, such as creamy truffle sauce or hearty meat ragu, Istrian fuži are a staple of local gastronomy.

Fritule

Treat your sweet tooth to fritule, traditional Croatian doughnuts that are popular throughout Istria and Dalmatia. Made with flour, eggs, sugar, and citrus zest, fritule are deep-fried until golden brown and crispy, then dusted with powdered sugar for a touch of sweetness.

Homemade pastries

Treat yourself to the irresistible flavours of homemade pastries, a beloved tradition in Labin's culinary culture. From flaky strudels filled with seasonal fruits to decadent chocolate tortes and delicate almond biscuits, Labin's pastry shops offer an array of sweet delights to satisfy any craving. Enjoy a leisurely afternoon sampling an assortment of homemade pastries paired with freshly brewed coffee or aromatic herbal tea, and indulge in the simple pleasures of Istrian hospitality and culinary craftsmanship.

Grilled seafood

Indulge in a seafood feast with Labin's array of grilled seafood dishes, showcasing the freshest catches from the Adriatic Sea. From succulent grilled fish fillets and plump prawns to tender calamari and flavourful shellfish, Labin's seafood restaurants offer a diverse selection of grilled specialties cooked to perfection over an open flame. Pair your grilled seafood with local olive oil, garlic, and herbs for a taste of authentic Istrian cuisine, and savour the flavours of the sea in every bite.

Istrian ham

Delight in the savoury flavours of Istrian ham, a cherished delicacy made from carefully cured pork hind legs. Known for its rich, smoky aroma and tender texture, Istrian ham is traditionally dry-cured with sea salt, herbs, and spices, then aged for several months to develop its distinct flavour profile.

Herb-infused liqueurs

Indulge in the vibrant flavours of herb-infused liqueurs, a traditional Croatian spirit crafted with locally sourced herbs, fruits, and spices. In Labin, you'll find a variety of artisanal liqueurs made from aromatic herbs such as sage, rosemary, and mint, as well as fruits like cherries, figs, and citrus.

Cheese platter

Explore the rich diversity of Istrian cheeses with a cheese platter featuring an assortment of artisanal cheeses crafted by local producers. From creamy goat cheese and tangy sheep's milk cheese to aged cow's milk cheese infused with truffles or herbs,

Labin's cheese platters offer a delightful journey through Istria's cheese-making heritage. Accompanied by freshly baked bread, homemade jams, and seasonal fruits, a cheese platter is the perfect way to experience the flavours and textures of Istrian cheeses in a single tasting.

As the sun sets over the rolling hills of Istria, Labin invites you to experience the true flavours of the region through its culinary delights. From savoury prosciutto to fragrant truffles and hearty soups, each dish tells a story of tradition, heritage, and the bountiful land that has shaped Istrian cuisine for centuries. Join us in savouring the tastes of Labin and discover why Istrian gastronomy is celebrated around the world.

Labin's enigmatic charms: Secrets along the shoreline

Beyond its well-known landmarks lie secret spots and off-the-beaten-path treasures that offer a glimpse into the town's rich history, culture, and natural beauty. From hidden chapels and secluded beaches to charming alleyways and panoramic viewpoints, Labin's hidden gems invite visitors to explore its hidden corners and uncover the essence of this enchanting town.

Vela Grabica beach

Tucked away along Labin's coastline, Vela Grabica Beach offers a serene retreat from the bustling crowds. Accessible via a winding path through lush Mediterranean vegetation, this hidden gem boasts crystal-clear waters and smooth pebbles, perfect for a quiet swim or basking in the sun's warmth.

Graffiti tunnel

Dive into Labin's urban art scene at the Graffiti Tunnel, an underground passageway adorned with vibrant street art and colourful murals. Spanning the length of the old town walls, this hidden gem serves as a canvas for local and international artists, showcasing a diverse range of styles and themes. From abstract compositions to social commentary, the artwork in the Graffiti Tunnel reflects Labin's creative spirit and contemporary culture, offering a unique and immersive experience for art enthusiasts

Jay Chandarana

St. John the Baptist chapel

Nestled within Labin's medieval core, the St. John the Baptist Chapel stands as a testament to the town's rich history and religious heritage. Dating back to the 15th century, this hidden gem features exquisite frescoes depicting biblical scenes and ornate altars adorned with intricate carvings.

Ploce beach cove

Venture off the beaten path to discover Ploce Beach Cove, a secluded paradise nestled along Labin's rugged coastline. Accessible only by foot or boat, this hidden gem offers pristine turquoise waters, surrounded by towering cliffs and lush greenery. Visitors can soak up the sun on the smooth pebble shoreline or explore the underwater world while snorkelling in the crystal-clear sea.

Gornji Grad lookout

Ascend to the heights of Gornji Grad and discover a hidden vantage point offering breath-taking views of Labin's rooftops, the shimmering Adriatic Sea, and the verdant Istrian countryside. Accessed via a labyrinth of cobblestone streets and stone staircases, this panoramic lookout rewards intrepid explorers with sweeping vistas and unparalleled photo opportunities.

Trget harbour

Discover the picturesque fishing village of Trget, hidden along Labin's coastline, where time seems to stand still amid its tranquil harbour and rustic charm. Surrounded by rocky cliffs and emerald waters, Trget offers a glimpse into traditional Istrian coastal life, with colourful fishing boats bobbing in the harbour and fishermen mending nets on the quayside. Visitors can savour freshly caught seafood at waterfront taverns, where the day's catch is grilled to perfection and served with local wine and olive oil.

Labin mine museum

Uncover the industrial heritage of Labin at the Labin Mine Museum, housed within the historic Dubrova Park. This hidden gem offers a fascinating journey into the town's mining past, showcasing the tools, machinery, and artifacts used in the extraction of coal and minerals from the surrounding hills. Visitors can descend into the depths of a simulated mine shaft, experiencing the sights and sounds of a working mine first-hand.

Vela Draga

Explore the natural wonders of Vela Draga, a hidden canyon nestled in the hinterlands of Labin. This secluded gem offers breath-taking vistas of towering limestone cliffs, lush forests, and meandering streams, creating an idyllic setting for outdoor adventures. Hikers can follow scenic trails that wind through the canyon, passing by hidden caves, cascading waterfalls, and ancient rock formations.

Gracisce

Step back in time and discover the medieval charm of Gracisce, a hidden hilltop village located just a short drive from Labin. Perched atop a verdant hillside, Gracisce boasts narrow cobblestone streets, ancient stone houses, and panoramic views of the Istrian countryside. Visitors can wander through the village's winding alleys, admiring historic churches, quaint squares, and centuries-old architecture at every turn.

Cave vrelo

Delve into the subterranean world of Cave Vrelo, a hidden natural wonder located near the village of Polje, just a short drive from Labin. This underground cave system features mesmerizing stalactites, stalagmites, and crystalline formations, illuminated by soft ambient lighting to enhance their beauty. Visitors can embark on guided tours of the cave, exploring its winding passages and cavernous chambers while learning about its geological history and formation.

Fortica castle

Discover the historic legacy of Fortica Castle, a hidden gem perched atop a hill overlooking the town of Labin. Dating back to the medieval period, this imposing fortress offers commanding views of the surrounding landscape and the shimmering waters of the Adriatic Sea. Visitors can explore the castle's well-preserved ramparts, bastions, and towers, imagining the battles and sieges that once took place within its walls.

As the sun sets over Labin's hidden gems, visitors depart with memories of secret beaches, artistic alleys, ancient chapels, panoramic vistas, and secluded gardens, each offering a glimpse into the town's unique charm and allure. These hidden treasures enrich the visitor experience, inviting exploration and discovery beyond the well-trodden paths of Labin's main attractions.

Thrills in nature: Labin's outdoor escapes unleashed

From rugged mountain trails to crystal-clear waters, Labin offers a diverse array of outdoor activities to suit every taste and preference. Whether you are seeking adrenaline-pumping thrills or peaceful moments of serenity, this charming town provides the perfect backdrop for unforgettable outdoor experiences.

Hiking in Ucka nature park

Explore the pristine wilderness of Učka Nature Park, located just a short drive from Labin. With its network of well-marked hiking trails, ranging from easy strolls to challenging treks, the park offers endless opportunities for outdoor exploration. Hikers can traverse lush forests, rugged peaks, and panoramic viewpoints, immersing themselves in the region's breath-taking natural beauty.

Cycling along Parenzana trail

Embark on a scenic cycling adventure along the Parenzana Trail, a historic railway route that winds its way through the Istrian countryside. This picturesque trail traverses vineyards, olive groves, and quaint villages, providing cyclists with stunning views at every turn.

Rock climbing in Rabac

Channel your inner adventurer and test your climbing skills on the rugged cliffs of Rabac, a coastal town known for its spectacular seaside scenery. With its towering limestone cliffs and crystal-clear waters, Rabac offers a thrilling playground for rock climbers of all abilities.

Sea Kayaking along the Istrian coast

Embark on an unforgettable sea kayaking expedition along the pristine coastline of Istria, starting from the charming town of Labin. Paddle through hidden coves, secluded beaches, and crystal-clear waters as you explore the region's stunning maritime landscapes.

Snorkelling and diving in Rabac

Dive into the underwater world of Rabac and discover an abundance of marine life thriving beneath the surface of the Adriatic Sea. With its clear waters, vibrant coral reefs, and diverse marine ecosystems, Rabac offers an exceptional snorkelling and diving experience for nature lovers and adventure seekers alike.

Off-road jeep safari in Labin countryside

Embark on an exhilarating off-road jeep safari adventure through the rugged countryside surrounding Labin. Traverse winding dirt roads, ancient forests, and remote villages as you discover the hidden gems of Istria's interior. Led by experienced guides, this adrenaline-pumping excursion offers a unique opportunity to explore off-the-beaten-path destinations and witness the region's stunning natural beauty up close.

Stand-up paddleboarding in Rabac bay

Experience the serene waters of Rabac Bay from a different perspective with stand-up paddleboarding. Glide across the calm sea surface, soaking in panoramic views of the surrounding coastline and distant islands. Whether you are a seasoned paddleboarder or a beginner looking to try something new, Rabac Bay's tranquil waters provide the perfect setting for a relaxing and scenic paddleboarding excursion.

Picnic in nature reserves

Escape the hustle and bustle of the town and enjoy a leisurely picnic in one of Labin's picturesque nature reserves. Pack a delicious spread of local delicacies and head to scenic spots such as Dubrova Park or Skitača Nature Reserve, where you can dine al fresco amidst stunning natural surroundings.

Caving expeditions in the Labin Karst

Delve into the mysterious underground world of the Labin Karst on an unforgettable caving expedition. Led by experienced guides, explore ancient cave systems, underground rivers, and fascinating rock formations hidden beneath the surface. Discover stalactites, stalagmites, and other geological wonders as you venture deep into the earth, uncovering the secrets of Istria's karst landscape.

Zip line adventures in Glavani park

Experience the thrill of flying through the air on a zip line adventure at Glavani Park, located near Labin. Strap into a harness and soar across lush green valleys, dense forests, and scenic landscapes, enjoying panoramic views of the Istrian countryside below.

Horseback riding excursions in Labin countryside

Saddle up and explore the picturesque countryside surrounding Labin on a horseback riding excursion. Ride through rolling hills, lush meadows, and ancient forests, immersing yourself in the tranquillity of nature while admiring panoramic views of the Adriatic Sea.

As the sun sets on your outdoor adventures in Labin, take a moment to reflect on the unforgettable experiences and natural wonders you've encountered along the way. From hiking through pristine forests to kayaking along scenic coastlines, Labin offers a wealth of outdoor activities that allow you to connect with nature and create cherished memories that will last a lifetime. Whether you are seeking adrenaline-fueled thrills or peaceful moments of serenity, Labin invites you to explore its breath-taking landscapes and embark on new adventures in the great outdoors.

Cultural Extravaganza: Festivals in Labin's Coastal Haven

Throughout the year, Labin comes alive with a variety of cultural events and festivals that showcase the town's rich heritage and artistic spirit. From music and art to religious rituals and historical commemorations, these festivities offer visitors a unique opportunity to experience the authentic culture and community spirit of Labin.

Labin Jazz Festival (June)

The 'Labin Jazz Festival' brings together renowned jazz musicians from Croatia and around the world for a series of electrifying performances in Labin's historic Old Town. From smooth melodies to improvisational solos, the festival showcases the diversity and talent of the jazz genre, attracting music enthusiasts of all ages to the charming streets and squares of Labin.

Festa sv. Florijana (May)

Dedicated to the patron saint of firefighters, the Feast of St. Floran is a traditional religious celebration held in the village of Vinež near Labin. The festivities include a solemn Mass, processions, live music, traditional dances, and culinary delights, bringing together locals and visitors to honour the saint and enjoy the vibrant atmosphere of the festival.

Dan Labinske Republike (March)

Commemorating Labin's unique history as a self-proclaimed independent republic during World War II, Labin Republic Day is a festive occasion marked by parades, re-enactments, historical exhibitions, and traditional ceremonies. Visitors can learn about the town's revolutionary past and join in the celebrations, experiencing the spirit of freedom and unity that defines Labin's identity.

Ljetni festival u Labinu (June to August)

During the summer months, Labin hosts a diverse array of cultural events and performances as part of the Labin Summer Festival. From open-air concerts and theatrical productions to art exhibitions and film screenings, this festival offers something for everyone to enjoy. Visitors can mingle with locals and immerse themselves in the lively atmosphere of the town's historic centre, making unforgettable memories under the Istrian sun.

Labin Street Art Festival (June)

Transforming the walls and alleyways of Labin into an open-air gallery, the Labin Street Art Festival invites local and international artists to create vibrant murals and installations throughout the town. From colourful graffiti to thought-provoking sculptures, the festival adds a contemporary twist to Labin's historic streetscape, inspiring dialogue and reflection among residents and visitors alike.

Festival istarskih priča (July)

Celebrating the rich folklore and oral traditions of Istria, the Festival of Istrian Folk Tales invites storytellers, musicians, and artists to Labin to share tales of local legends and myths. Through captivating performances and interactive workshops, attendees can learn about Istrian culture and heritage while enjoying the enchanting ambiance of the festival.

Labin Svibanj (April)

Festival prirode i baštine): Held in the picturesque surroundings of Labin's countryside, the Labin Spring festival celebrates the beauty of nature and the region's rich cultural heritage. Visitors can explore hiking trails, visit archaeological sites, and participate in eco-friendly activities such as tree planting and nature conservation workshops.

Eko Ethno Festival (August)

Embracing the principles of sustainability and cultural diversity, the Eco Ethno Festival in Labin celebrates the harmonious coexistence of nature and tradition. Through workshops, exhibitions, and performances, the festival promotes eco-friendly practices and showcases the traditional crafts, music, and cuisine of Istria.

Festival vina i gastronomije (October)

Wine lovers and foodies converge in Labin for the annual Wine & Gastronomy Festival, where they can savour the flavours of Istrian cuisine and sample the region's finest wines. Local winemakers and chefs showcase their products through tastings, workshops, and culinary demonstrations, offering insights into Istria's rich gastronomic heritage.

Labin Rock Festival (August)

Rock music enthusiasts gather in Labin for an electrifying weekend of live performances and outdoor concerts at the Labin Rock Festival. Featuring both established and up-and-coming bands from Croatia and abroad, the festival showcases a diverse range of rock genres, from classic and alternative rock to punk and metal.

Whether honoring its revolutionary past or celebrating contemporary art and music, Labin's festivals and events serve as a testament to the town's enduring spirit and sense of community. As visitors bid farewell to Labin's lively streets and welcoming atmosphere, they carry with them memories of unforgettable experiences and the warm hospitality of this charming Istrian town.

Insider's guide: Navigating Labin's coastal charms

With its rich history, charming architecture, and stunning natural landscapes, Labin is a hidden gem waiting to be explored. Whether you are wandering through its medieval streets, soaking up the sun on its pristine beaches, or indulging in its delicious cuisine, Labin offers something for every traveller. To make the most of your visit, here are some travel tips to help you navigate this enchanting destination.

Explore the old town

Wander through Labin's labyrinthine streets and admire the well-preserved medieval architecture that characterizes the Old Town. The narrow cobblestone alleys are lined with colourful houses adorned with traditional wooden shutters and intricate stonework.

Hike or bike in nature

Labin's scenic surroundings offer ample opportunities for outdoor exploration. Lace up your hiking boots and hit the trails that wind through lush forests, rolling hills, and vineyard-covered slopes. Alternatively, rent a bike and embark on a cycling adventure along the Istrian Peninsula's network of well-marked bike paths, which offer stunning views of the coastline and the surrounding countryside.

Discover the mining heritage

Labin's mining heritage is an integral part of its identity, and visitors can delve into this history at the Labin National Museum. Explore the exhibits detailing the town's mining past, including artifacts, photographs, and interactive displays that provide insight into the lives of the miners who once worked in the region's coal mines.

Take a guided tour

To gain a deeper understanding of Labin's history and culture, consider joining a guided tour led by knowledgeable locals. These tours often include visits to key landmarks and attractions, as well as insightful commentary on the town's fascinating past.

Shop for local crafts

Support local artisans and take home a piece of Labin's culture by browsing the shops and galleries that line the streets of the Old Town. From handcrafted ceramics and pottery to intricate lacework and embroidery, you'll find a variety of unique souvenirs that showcase the region's traditional craftsmanship.

Explore the surrounding villages

Venture beyond the confines of Labin to discover the charming villages and countryside that surround the town. Take a scenic drive through the rolling hills of Istria, stopping to explore picturesque villages like Vinez, known for its wine production, and Kršan, home to a stunning hilltop castle.

Relax in nature

Escape the hustle and bustle of everyday life and reconnect with nature in Labin's pristine surroundings. Pack a picnic and head to one of the area's idyllic parks or nature reserves, where you can enjoy leisurely walks, scenic picnics, and birdwatching amidst lush greenery.

Visit art galleries

Explore Labin's thriving art scene by visiting its numerous galleries and studios showcasing the works of local artists. Admire contemporary paintings, sculptures, and installations that reflect the region's rich cultural heritage and artistic legacy.

Engage in outdoor adventures

For outdoor enthusiasts, Labin offers a wealth of activities to enjoy amidst its stunning natural surroundings. Hike or bike along scenic trails that wind through forests, valleys, and coastal paths, offering breath-taking views at every turn. Alternatively, embark on a thrilling adventure with activities like rock climbing, zip-lining, or off-road excursions that promise adrenaline-pumping fun for adventurers of all levels.

As you bid farewell to Labin, take with you memories of its historic charm, scenic beauty, and warm hospitality. Whether you are a history buff, a nature lover, or a foodie, Labin has something to offer every traveller. With these travel tips in hand, you are sure to make the most of your time in this enchanting destination and create unforgettable experiences that will last a lifetime.

Until we meet again: Labin's coastal legacy lingers on

As you conclude your exploration of Labin, a town steeped in history and culture, take a moment to reflect on the memories you've created and the experiences you've savoured. Labin's rich cultural heritage, from its historic Old Town to its vibrant art scene, leaves an indelible mark on visitors, inviting them to immerse themselves in its rich tapestry of traditions and creativity. The warmth of the locals, the flavours of its culinary delights, and the beauty of its coastal landscapes combine to create a lasting impression that lingers long after you've bid farewell to this enchanting hilltop town.

In Labin, every cobblestone street, every historic building, and every art installation holds a story waiting to be discovered. As you carry the essence of Labin with you, may the memories of its cultural riches, culinary delights, and natural wonders continue to inspire and captivate your heart, reminding you of the beauty and magic found in this hidden gem along Croatia's Istrian coast. Whether it is the echoes of ancient civilizations, the taste of fresh seafood, or the sight of a stunning sunset over the Adriatic Sea, Labin's closing thoughts are a symphony of experiences that resonate with the soul and beckon you to return to its embrace.

Cavtat: Jewel of the Riviera

Coastal escape: Cavtat's Adriatic charms in tranquil bliss

With its cobbled streets and sun-kissed shores, Cavtat unfolds like a timeless tale along the Adriatic coast. Steeped in history and adorned with architectural marvels, this coastal gem captivates the imagination of all who wander its lanes. From the ancient ruins that whisper tales of bygone eras to the bustling harbour where fishing boats bob gently in the breeze, Cavtat exudes an irresistible allure that invites exploration and discovery.

As the sun sets over the horizon, painting the sky in hues of orange and pink, Cavtat comes alive with the rhythms of coastal life. Locals and visitors alike gather along the promenade, savouring the moment as day gives way to night. The scent of fresh seafood mingles with the sound of laughter and music, creating an atmosphere of warmth and conviviality. In Cavtat, every moment is a celebration of the simple joys of life, where time seems to stand still amidst the beauty of the Adriatic coastline

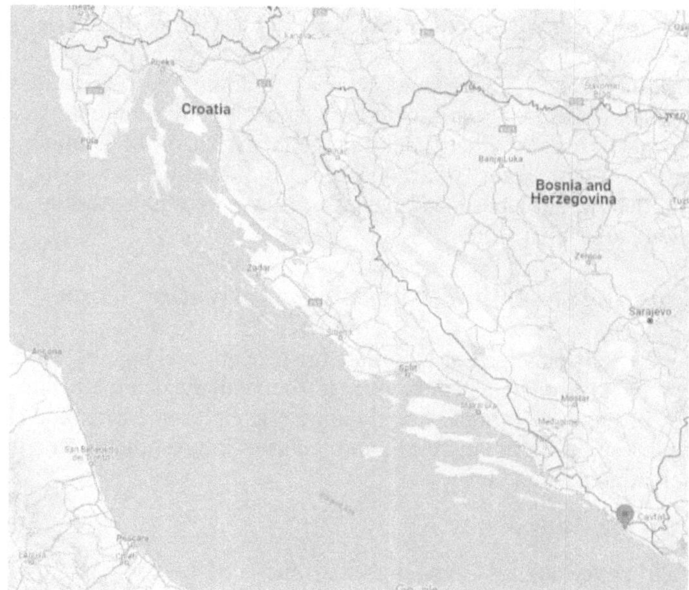

Adriatic sentinel: Cavtat's maritime legacy revealed

Cavtat's historical significance spans millennia, tracing back to its origins as the ancient Greek settlement of Epidaurum. Over the centuries, it flourished under Roman rule, serving as an important maritime and trading centre in the Adriatic. Its strategic location attracted various civilizations, from the Byzantines to the Venetians, each leaving their mark on its cultural landscape. The remnants of ancient villas, Roman baths, and medieval fortifications bear witness to Cavtat's rich and diverse history, offering glimpses into its storied past.

In addition to its ancient heritage, Cavtat played a pivotal role in the development of Croatian culture and identity. As one of the oldest settlements in the region, it served as a hub for art, literature, and commerce, fostering creativity and innovation among its inhabitants. Notable figures such as the renowned painter Vlaho Bukovac and the celebrated poet and playwright Vlaho Paljetak were born in Cavtat, leaving a lasting legacy that continues to inspire generations to this day. As visitors explore its historic streets and landmarks, they are transported back in time, connecting with the rich tapestry of Cavtat's heritage and its enduring significance in Croatian history.

Cultural oasis: Cavtat's Mediterranean soul revealed

Cavtat's local culture is a vibrant tapestry woven with traditions, customs, and a deep appreciation for the beauty of life along the Adriatic coast. From its rich maritime heritage to its lively festivals and artistic community, the town exudes an atmosphere of warmth and hospitality that welcomes visitors with open arms. Fishermen ply the waters in colourful boats, bringing in the day's catch to be enjoyed in the local taverns, where fresh seafood dishes are savoured alongside glasses of local wine.

Art and music are integral parts of Cavtat's cultural identity, with galleries showcasing the works of talented local artists and street performers adding a touch of melody to the town's bustling streets. Throughout the year, traditional festivals and celebrations honour age-old customs and rituals, offering visitors a glimpse into the heart and soul of Cavtat's local culture. Whether joining in the festivities of the Summer Carnival or experiencing the solemn beauty of St. Nicholas Day, travellers are invited to immerse themselves in the vibrant tapestry of Cavtat's cultural traditions, forging connections that endure long after their visit.

Jewels along the shoreline: Adriatic's captivating icons

Welcome to Cavtat, a picturesque coastal town nestled along the Adriatic Sea in southern Croatia. Steeped in history and surrounded by natural beauty, Cavtat is renowned for its charming Old Town, stunning seaside promenade, and rich cultural heritage. Explore a wealth of landmarks and points of interest that offer a glimpse into Cavtat's fascinating past and present.

Mausoleum of the Racic family

Perched on a hill overlooking Cavtat, the Mausoleum of the Racic Family is a striking example of modernist architecture. Designed by renowned sculptor Ivan Meštrović in the early 20th century, the mausoleum is a tribute to the influential Racic family, who played a significant role in Cavtat's cultural and economic development.

Cavtat seaside promenade

Stretching along the azure waters of the Adriatic, the Cavtat Seaside Promenade is a scenic thoroughfare that invites visitors to bask in the town's coastal charm. Lined with palm trees, cafes, and boutiques, the promenade offers a leisurely stroll with stunning views of the harbour and nearby islands. From sunrise to sunset, it is a favourite spot for locals and tourists alike to enjoy the sea breeze and soak up the Mediterranean ambiance.

House of Vlaho Bukovac

Discover the life and works of one of Croatia's most celebrated artists at the House of Vlaho Bukovac. Situated in a historic building overlooking the town, this museum offers a glimpse into the world of Vlaho Bukovac, known for his vibrant portraits and landscapes. Explore the artist's former residence, adorned with his paintings, sketches, and personal belongings, and gain insight into his artistic journey and legacy in Cavtat.

Fortress of Rat

Perched atop a hill overlooking Cavtat's harbour, the Fortress of Rat offers commanding views of the Adriatic Sea and the surrounding coastline. Dating back to the 15th century, this historic fortress served as a defensive stronghold against maritime threats during the time of the Republic of Ragusa. Today, visitors can explore its ancient walls and towers, immersing themselves in Cavtat's military history while enjoying panoramic vistas of the town and its scenic surroundings.

Franciscan monastery and church of Our Lady of the snow

Situated near Cavtat's main square, the Franciscan Monastery and Church of Our Lady of the Snow are architectural treasures that have stood the test of time. Founded in the 15th century, the monastery boasts a Renaissance cloister adorned with intricate stone carvings and a peaceful courtyard garden. The adjacent church features a stunning Baroque altar and a collection of valuable artworks, offering visitors a glimpse into Cavtat's religious heritage and cultural legacy.

Rector's palace

Built in the 16th century during the time of the Republic of Ragusa, the Rector's Palace stands as a testament to Cavtat's Renaissance heritage. Its elegant facade and Venetian-style architecture make it a prominent landmark in the town. Inside, visitors can admire a collection of historical artifacts and artworks, providing insight into Cavtat's political and cultural significance during the medieval period.

St. Roch's church

Nestled in the heart of Cavtat's historic centre, St. Roch's Church is a charming architectural gem that dates back to the 15th century. Named after the patron saint of plague victims, the church features a simple yet elegant facade and a serene interior adorned with religious artworks and sacred relics.

Cavtat promenade

Stretching along the picturesque coastline, the Cavtat Promenade is a vibrant hub of activity where locals and visitors alike come to stroll, relax, and soak in the seaside atmosphere. Lined with palm trees, cafes, and charming boutiques, the promenade offers stunning views of the Adriatic Sea and Cavtat's scenic harbour.

Cavtat art gallery

Located in a historic villa overlooking the sea, the Cavtat Art Gallery is a cultural treasure trove showcasing the works of prominent Croatian artists from the 19th and 20th centuries. The gallery's extensive collection includes paintings, sculptures, and other artworks that highlight Cavtat's rich artistic heritage and creative spirit.

Jay Chandarana

Memorial house of Baltazar Bogisic

This museum is dedicated to Baltazar Bogisic, a prominent Croatian jurist and legal scholar who made significant contributions to the field of comparative law. Housed in a traditional stone building in Cavtat's old town, the museum showcases Bogišić's personal library, manuscripts, and memorabilia, providing insights into his life and intellectual legacy. Visitors can explore exhibits highlighting Bogišić's pioneering work in legal studies and his enduring impact on Croatian jurisprudence and legal education.

Church of St. Nicholas

Dominating the town's skyline with its distinctive Baroque bell tower, the Church of St. Nicholas is one of Cavtat's most revered religious sites. Originally constructed in the 15th century, the church underwent several renovations over the centuries, resulting in its current grandeur. Inside, visitors can marvel at the intricate altars, ornate frescoes, and relics housed within its sacred walls, offering a glimpse into Cavtat's spiritual traditions.

As you explore the enchanting town of Cavtat, you'll discover a tapestry of historical landmarks and cultural treasures that showcase its rich heritage. From centuries-old churches to scenic seaside promenades, Cavtat offers a wealth of experiences that will leave you enchanted by its beauty and history. Embrace the allure of this coastal gem and let its timeless charm captivate your heart.

Epicurean adventures: Exploring tastes of the destination

Discover the unique flavours of Cavtat, where traditional Croatian cuisine meets coastal delicacies. Embark on a culinary journey through its charming streets and waterfront eateries, indulging in dishes that reflect the rich cultural heritage of this seaside town.

Ston oysters

Renowned for their exceptional quality and distinctive flavour profile, Ston oysters are a culinary treasure of Cavtat. Grown in the pristine waters of the nearby Pelješac Peninsula, these briny bivalves boast a unique combination of sweetness and minerality.

Brodetto

A beloved dish along the Adriatic coast, brodetto is a hearty seafood stew that reflects the maritime heritage of Cavtat. Brimming with an abundance of locally sourced fish, including scorpionfish, monkfish, and sea bass, the stew is simmered to perfection in a rich tomato-based broth infused with garlic, onions, and aromatic herbs. Served with a side of polenta or crusty bread, brodetto is a soul-warming dish that evokes memories of seaside dining and coastal living.

Fig Delights

Indulge your sweet tooth with a taste of Cavtat's fig delights, a beloved delicacy that celebrates the abundance of ripe, succulent figs harvested from the region's orchards. From fig jam and preserves to stuffed figs and fig-infused desserts, there are endless ways to enjoy this versatile fruit. Experience the luscious sweetness and subtle earthiness of Cavtat's figs in a variety of culinary creations.

Soparnik

Delight in a taste of Dalmatian heritage with soparnik, a savoury pie that dates back centuries in Croatian cuisine. Made from simple ingredients such as Swiss chard, garlic, and olive oil, layered between thin sheets of dough, soparnik is baked to golden perfection, resulting in a crispy exterior and a tender, flavourful filling. Enjoyed as a hearty snack or appetizer, soparnik embodies the rustic charm and culinary heritage of Cavtat, offering a delicious glimpse into the region's gastronomic traditions.

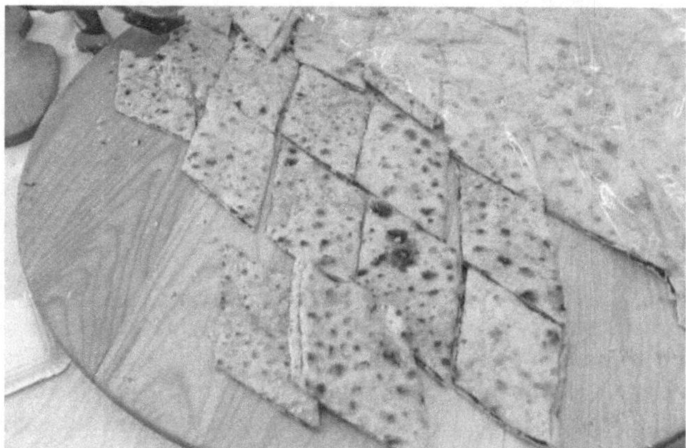

Herb-infused delicacies

Immerse yourself in the aromatic world of Cavtat's herb-infused delicacies, where fragrant herbs such as rosemary, lavender, and bay leaf impart their distinctive flavours to traditional dishes. Taste the essence of the Mediterranean landscape in dishes like herb-crusted lamb chops, lavender-infused desserts, and rosemary-scented olive oil.

Artisanal cheese

Tasting: Embark on a cheese-tasting journey in Cavtat, where artisanal cheesemakers craft a diverse array of cheeses from the rich milk of local sheep and goats. Sample aged sheep's milk cheeses like Paški sir and Dalmatinski sir, known for their distinct flavours and textures. Taste creamy goat cheeses infused with herbs, spices, and even truffles, adding complexity and depth to each bite. Learn about the cheesemaking process from passionate artisans who uphold traditional techniques and strive for excellence in every wheel of cheese.

Traditional bread making

Immerse yourself in the age-old tradition of bread making in Cavtat, where skilled bakers knead and bake artisanal bread using time-honoured techniques and locally sourced ingredients. Participate in a hands-on bread-making workshop and learn how to prepare dough from scratch, shape it into loaves, and bake it to golden perfection in a wood-fired oven. Experience the satisfaction of creating your own loaf of bread, infused with the aroma of freshly baked grains and the warmth of Cavtat's hospitality.

Rozata

No meal in Cavtat is complete without indulging in a slice of Rožata, a traditional Croatian custard pudding with a delightful twist. Made from a blend of eggs, sugar, milk, and citrus zest, Rožata is gently baked until set and then chilled to perfection. The pudding is then inverted onto a plate, revealing a smooth, creamy texture and a luscious caramel glaze.

As you explore the streets of Cavtat, let your taste buds guide you on a culinary adventure filled with unique flavours and unforgettable experiences. From the depths of the sea to the heart of Dalmatia, each dish offers a glimpse into the culinary heritage of this enchanting coastal town. With its diverse array of flavours and ingredients, Cavtat invites you to savour the essence of Croatian cuisine amidst its scenic beauty.

Revealing mysteries: Delving into Cavtat's intriguing secrets

Welcome to Cavtat, a picturesque coastal town nestled along the Adriatic coast of Croatia. While its historic charm and stunning natural beauty are well-known, Cavtat also hides away some hidden gems waiting to be discovered by intrepid travellers. From secluded beaches to hidden viewpoints and secret gardens, these hidden gems offer a glimpse into the quieter, more authentic side of Cavtat.

Kljucice beach

Escape the crowds and discover the hidden oasis of Ključice Beach, located just a short walk from Cavtat's town centre. This secluded stretch of coastline offers crystal-clear waters, smooth pebbles, and plenty of shade from towering pine trees. Perfect for a peaceful day of swimming, sunbathing, or simply unwinding amidst the natural beauty of the Adriatic coast.

Bukovac house

Step back in time and explore the hidden gem of Bukovac House, a museum dedicated to the life and work of renowned Croatian painter Vlaho Bukovac. Tucked away in the heart of Cavtat's old town, this charming house-museum showcases Bukovac's vibrant artworks, personal belongings, and studio space. Visitors can wander through the artist's former home and gain insight into his creative process and artistic legacy.

Ljuta river

Venture off the beaten path and discover the tranquil beauty of Ljuta River, a hidden gem nestled in the lush greenery of Cavtat's hinterland. Follow the meandering river as it winds its way through verdant landscapes, passing by old stone mills and rustic watermills along the way.

Rat peninsula

Explore the secluded Rat Peninsula, a hidden gem located just a short boat ride from Cavtat's harbour. This pristine coastal area boasts rugged cliffs, hidden coves, and unspoiled nature, making it a paradise for nature lovers and outdoor enthusiasts. Take a leisurely hike along the scenic trails that crisscross the peninsula, stopping to admire breath-taking views of the Adriatic Sea and nearby islands.

Racic mausoleum

Tucked away amidst lush Mediterranean vegetation, the Račić Mausoleum is a hidden architectural gem in Cavtat. Designed by renowned Croatian sculptor Ivan Meštrović, this elegant mausoleum is dedicated to the Račić family and features intricate stone carvings and striking geometric patterns. Visitors can admire the serene beauty of this monument while soaking in panoramic views of the Adriatic Sea and Cavtat's scenic coastline.

Bacan beach

For a truly secluded beach experience, venture to Bacan Beach, hidden away from the main tourist areas of Cavtat. Accessible only by boat or a rugged coastal trail, this hidden gem offers pristine pebble shores, clear turquoise waters, and stunning views of the surrounding coastline.

Vlaho Bukovac art gallery

Delve into Cavtat's artistic heritage at the Vlaho Bukovac Art Gallery, a hidden gem located within the historic walls of the town. Housed in a charming stone building, this gallery showcases the works of renowned Croatian painter Vlaho Bukovac, as well as other local artists. Explore the diverse collection of paintings, sculptures, and contemporary artworks, and gain insight into Cavtat's rich cultural heritage.

Pasjaca beach

Hidden at the bottom of a dramatic cliffside staircase lies Pasjača Beach, a hidden gem known for its stunning natural beauty. Carved into the rugged coastline, this secluded beach boasts crystal-clear waters, golden sands, and breath-taking views of the Adriatic Sea. While the descent to the beach may be challenging, the reward of tranquillity and serenity makes it well worth the effort.

Cavtat old town walls

Escape the crowds and explore the hidden corners of Cavtat's Old Town Walls, which offer panoramic views of the town and surrounding coastline. Follow the winding pathways along the ancient fortifications, passing by hidden gardens, charming churches, and historic landmarks along the way.

As the sun sets on your adventures in Cavtat, take a moment to reflect on the hidden gems you've discovered along the way. From hidden beaches and historic monuments to tranquil rivers and scenic viewpoints, these hidden treasures add depth and richness to Cavtat's already enchanting allure. Whether you are seeking solitude, serenity, or simply a sense of wonder, Cavtat's hidden gems promise unforgettable experiences and cherished memories for all who seek them.

Exploring nature's bounty: Outdoor pursuits in Cavtat

Write me info for the town Labin on the following topic-'Outdoor activities', as many as you can for my ebook where there will be title of the 'Outdoor activities', with description for each in 5 lines and also an intro paragraph along with a conclusion para of about 2-3 line.

Hiking trails

Lace up your hiking boots and venture into Cavtat's picturesque countryside, where a network of scenic trails awaits discovery. From leisurely walks to challenging treks, there are routes suitable for all skill levels, offering opportunities to immerse yourself in nature's beauty. Traverse lush forests, ascend rugged hillsides, and be rewarded with breath-taking vistas of the Adriatic Sea and surrounding landscapes along the way.

Snorkelling and diving

Dive into the vibrant underwater world of the Adriatic Sea with snorkelling and diving excursions available in Cavtat. Explore colourful coral reefs, encounter diverse marine life, and marvel at ancient shipwrecks resting on the seabed.

Boat tours and island hopping

Set sail on a boat tour from Cavtat's harbour and embark on an island-hopping adventure to nearby isles and hidden gems of the Adriatic coast. Visit picturesque islands, swim in secluded bays, and soak up the Mediterranean sun aboard a traditional wooden boat or modern catamaran.

Cycling Adventures

Discover Cavtat's scenic countryside on two wheels with cycling adventures that cater to all levels of riders. Pedal along coastal roads, meander through olive groves and vineyards, and explore charming villages nestled in the hillsides.

Stand-up Paddleboarding (SUP

Glide across the calm waters of Cavtat Bay on a stand-up paddleboard and enjoy a unique perspective of the town's scenic coastline. Perfect for beginners and experienced paddlers alike, SUP allows you to explore hidden coves, navigate through sea caves, and even practice yoga on your board for a tranquil experience on the water.

Fishing Excursions

Join a fishing excursion and cast your line into the Adriatic Sea, where abundant marine life awaits. Whether you are a seasoned angler or trying fishing for the first time, Cavtat offers various fishing tours catered to different preferences. Spend a relaxing day at sea, reel in your catch of the day, and enjoy the thrill of the hunt surrounded by stunning coastal views.

Parasailing

Experience the exhilarating sensation of flying high above the Adriatic Sea with a parasailing adventure in Cavtat. Strap into a harness, ascend into the sky, and marvel at panoramic views of the coastline and surrounding islands below. With the wind in your hair and the sea breeze on your face, parasailing offers an unforgettable aerial perspective of Cavtat's natural beauty.

Rock Climbing

Test your strength and agility on Cavtat's rugged cliffs with rock climbing adventures suitable for climbers of all levels. Guided by experienced instructors, you'll scale limestone cliffs overlooking the Adriatic, surrounded by stunning coastal landscapes. Whether you are a beginner seeking a new challenge or a seasoned climber looking for adrenaline-fueled ascents, Cavtat's rock climbing opportunities provide thrilling experiences in a breath-taking setting.

Zip-lining

Soar through the treetops and experience the thrill of zip-lining in Cavtat's picturesque countryside. Zip across lush valleys, over crystal-clear streams, and through dense forests, enjoying bird's-eye views of the surrounding landscape. With exhilarating zip-line courses available, you'll embark on an adrenaline-pumping adventure while surrounded by Cavtat's natural beauty.

Sea Kayaking

Explore Cavtat's stunning coastline from a different perspective by embarking on a sea kayaking adventure. Paddle along the tranquil waters of the Adriatic Sea, discovering hidden caves, secluded beaches, and picturesque coves along the way. With the gentle sound of waves lapping against your kayak, you'll immerse yourself in the beauty of Cavtat's coastal scenery while enjoying a peaceful and environmentally friendly mode of exploration.

Mountain Biking

Hit the trails and discover Cavtat's rugged terrain on two wheels with a mountain biking excursion. Traverse forested paths, rocky trails, and scenic routes that wind through the town's surrounding hills and countryside. Whether you are an experienced cyclist seeking adrenaline-fueled descents or a leisure rider looking for picturesque routes, Cavtat offers biking adventures suitable for all skill levels, promising unforgettable experiences amid breath-taking landscapes.

Yacht Charter

Embark on a luxury yacht charter and sail the azure waters of the Adriatic Sea in style. Explore Cavtat's coastline and neighbouring islands aboard a private yacht, enjoying personalized service, gourmet cuisine, and breath-taking views of the Dalmatian coast. Whether you are seeking a romantic sunset cruise, a day of island hopping, or a week-long sailing adventure, Cavtat offers yacht charters tailored to your preferences, promising an unforgettable maritime experience.

As you immerse yourself in the outdoor activities of Cavtat, you'll discover a paradise for adventure enthusiasts and nature lovers alike. Whether you are kayaking along the coast, hiking through lush landscapes, or diving into the azure waters of the Adriatic, Cavtat's natural beauty and diverse terrain provide endless opportunities for exploration and excitement. With each outdoor adventure, you'll create unforgettable memories and forge a deeper connection with the stunning landscapes of this coastal gem.

Immersing in tradition: Festivals that define Cavtat's spirit

Immerse yourself in the vibrant culture and timeless traditions of Cavtat, a picturesque coastal town nestled along the Adriatic Sea in Croatia. Throughout the year, Cavtat comes alive with a variety of local festivals and celebrations that showcase the town's rich heritage and deep-rooted customs. From music and dance performances to culinary delights and cultural exhibitions, these events offer visitors a unique opportunity to experience the heart and soul of Cavtat's community.

Sveti Nikola (December)

Saint Nicholas Day is a beloved tradition in Cavtat, particularly among the local fishing community. On December 6th, the feast day of Saint Nicholas, the patron saint of sailors and fishermen, Cavtat comes alive with colourful processions and festivities. Boats decorated with festive lights and ornaments parade along the waterfront, while families gather to honour the saint and receive blessings for safe voyages and bountiful catches.

Festival Folklora (June)

The Folklore Festival in Cavtat is a celebration of Croatian folk music, dance, and traditional arts. Held annually in the town's historic squares and cultural venues, this festival brings together folk ensembles from across Croatia to showcase their unique regional dances, costumes, and musical traditions. Visitors can enjoy lively performances featuring intricate choreography, colourful costumes, and spirited music, providing insight into Croatia's rich cultural heritage.

Ljetni Umjetnički Festival u Cavtatu (July-August)

The Cavtat Summer Art Festival is a testament to the town's thriving arts scene and creative spirit. Featuring a diverse program of exhibitions, workshops, and performances, this festival celebrates the talents of local and international artists across various disciplines, including painting, sculpture, photography, and performance art.

Ribarski Dani u Cavtatu (July)

The Cavtat Fishermen's Days pay homage to the town's maritime heritage and the enduring traditions of its fishing community. Held annually during the summer months, this festival celebrates the bounty of the sea with a series of events and activities cantered around fishing, seafood, and maritime culture. Visitors can enjoy fresh seafood tastings, boat tours of the local fishing fleet, and demonstrations of traditional fishing techniques, providing insight into the daily lives of Cavtat's fishermen and their deep connection to the Adriatic Sea.

Ljetni Karneval u Cavtatu (August)

The Cavtat Summer Carnival brings joy and merriment to the streets of Cavtat with its colourful parades, elaborate costumes, and lively music. Held during the peak tourist season, this carnival celebration attracts locals and visitors alike, who come together to revel in the festive atmosphere. Participants don elaborate masks and costumes inspired by Croatian folklore and international themes, adding to the spectacle of the procession.

Uskrsni Običaji u Cavtatu (March/April)

Easter holds special significance in Cavtat, with the town's residents observing age-old traditions and customs to mark the occasion. From religious processions and church services to festive gatherings and family meals, Easter in Cavtat is a time of spiritual reflection, renewal, and community. Visitors can witness the solemn Good Friday processions through the town's streets, participate in Easter Sunday Mass at the local churches, and join in the joyful Easter Monday festivities, which often include egg hunts, picnics, and cultural performances.

Festival Berbe u Cavtatu (September)

The Cavtat Harvest Festival celebrates the bounty of the region's agricultural heritage and the rich flavours of its seasonal produce. Held in the early autumn, this festival brings together local farmers, artisans, and food enthusiasts to showcase the finest fruits, vegetables, and culinary delights of the harvest season. Visitors can sample freshly harvested produce, artisanal cheeses, homemade jams, and other gourmet treats, while enjoying live music, cultural performances, and agricultural exhibitions. The festival also offers opportunities to learn about traditional farming practices, sustainable agriculture, and the importance of preserving Croatia's agricultural heritage.

Festival Meda u Cavtatu (October)

The Cavtat Honey Festival celebrates the ancient tradition of beekeeping and the natural wonders of honey produced in the region. Held in late spring or early summer, this event brings together beekeepers, artisans, and honey enthusiasts for a day of honey-themed festivities and educational activities. Visitors can sample an array of locally harvested honeys, learn about the importance of bees in pollination and ecosystem health, and discover the various uses of honey in culinary and medicinal practices. The festival also features demonstrations of honey extraction, beeswax crafting, and traditional honey-based recipes, providing a sweet and enriching experience for all ages.

Likovna Kolonija u Cavtatu (May)

The Cavtat Art Colony is an annual gathering of artists from Croatia and around the world, who come together to create and exhibit their works in the scenic surroundings of Cavtat. Established in the early 20th century, the colony has a rich history of fostering creativity and artistic expression in various mediums, including painting, sculpture, and multimedia installations. Visitors can explore the colony's galleries and studios, attend artist talks and workshops, and even purchase original artworks to take home as souvenirs of their time in Cavtat.

Festival Lavande u Cavtatu (June)

The Cavtat Lavender Festival celebrates the fragrant blooms of lavender that blanket the countryside surrounding the town. Held in late spring or early summer, this event showcases the beauty and versatility of lavender through art displays, craft workshops, and culinary demonstrations. Visitors can explore lavender fields in full bloom, learn about the therapeutic properties of lavender essential oil, and sample lavender-infused delicacies such as honey, ice cream, and cocktails. The festival also features live music performances, cultural exhibits, and guided tours of local lavender farms, providing a sensory journey through the sights, scents, and flavours of Cavtat's lavender harvest.

From lively summer festivals to intimate cultural gatherings, each event offers a glimpse into Cavtat's unique identity and storied past. Whether you are savouring the flavours of Croatian cuisine at the Wine Festival or dancing in the streets during the Summer Carnival, these experiences will leave you with cherished memories and a deeper appreciation for Cavtat's cultural heritage.

Savvy traveller's handbook: Making memories in Cavtat

With its rich history, stunning natural beauty, and vibrant cultural scene, Cavtat offers a wealth of experiences for travellers seeking a unique and unforgettable holiday destination. Whether you are exploring ancient ruins, lounging on pristine beaches, or savouring local delicacies at seaside tavernas, Cavtat beckons with its irresistible allure and warm hospitality.

Explore the Old Town

Cavtat's Old Town is a labyrinth of narrow streets lined with charming stone houses, historic churches, and hidden squares. Take your time wandering through its winding alleys, stopping to admire architectural details and soaking in the atmosphere of centuries past. Do not miss landmarks like the Rector's Palace, an elegant Venetian-style building dating back to the 16th century, and the Church of St. Nicholas, with its striking bell tower and Baroque façade.

Take a Boat Trip

Set sail from Cavtat's harbour on a boat trip to discover the hidden treasures of the Adriatic Sea. Cruise along the coastline, passing rugged cliffs, secluded coves, and picturesque islands. Stop for a swim in crystal-clear waters, snorkel among colourful marine life, or simply relax on deck and soak up the Mediterranean sun.

Hike to the Ronald Brown Path

Lace up your hiking boots and embark on the Ronald Brown Path, a scenic trail that winds its way along the rugged coastline of Cavtat. Named after an American diplomat who loved the area, this trail offers breath-taking views of the Adriatic Sea and the lush greenery of the surrounding hillsides. Along the way, you'll encounter fragrant pine forests, ancient olive groves, and charming stone villages.

Visit the Racic Mausoleum

Perched on a hillside overlooking Cavtat, the Racic Mausoleum is a stunning architectural masterpiece designed by renowned sculptor Ivan Meštrović. Built in the early 20th century as a final resting place for the Racic family, this elegant mausoleum features intricate carvings, marble columns, and a domed roof adorned with symbolic motifs. Inside, you'll find beautiful sculptures and reliefs created by Meštrović himself, showcasing his exceptional talent and artistic vision.

Explore Lokrum Island

Just a short boat ride from Cavtat lies Lokrum Island, a nature reserve known for its lush vegetation, rocky beaches, and medieval ruins. Spend a day exploring the island's walking trails, botanical gardens, and historical landmarks, including the ruins of a Benedictine monastery and a Napoleonic fortress. Do not miss the opportunity to swim in the crystal-clear waters of Lokrum's secluded bays or relax in the shade of its pine groves.

Attend the Cavtat Summer Festival (Cavtatsko Ljeto)

Experience the vibrant cultural scene of Cavtat by attending the Cavtat Summer Festival, a month-long celebration of music, dance, theatre, and art. Held annually from mid-June to mid-July, the festival features performances by local and international artists in venues throughout the town, including open-air stages, historic squares, and waterfront promenades. Highlights of the festival include classical concerts, traditional folk dances, and contemporary theatre productions.

Take a Day Trip to Dubrovnik

Just a short drive or boat ride from Cavtat lies the historic city of Dubrovnik, a UNESCO World Heritage Site renowned for its well-preserved medieval walls, baroque architecture, and stunning coastal views. Spend a day exploring Dubrovnik's narrow streets and hidden alleyways, visiting iconic landmarks such as the Rector's Palace, the Cathedral of St. Blaise, and the Stradun, the city's main thoroughfare. Walk along the ancient city walls for panoramic views of the Adriatic Sea and the red-tiled rooftops below, or take a cable car ride to the top of Mount Srd for breath-taking vistas of the city and surrounding islands.

Experience Cavtat's Sunset

End your day in Cavtat with a spectacular sunset experience, as the sky is painted in shades of pink, orange, and gold. Find a cozy spot along the waterfront or climb to one of the town's scenic viewpoints to watch the sun dip below the horizon, casting a warm glow over the Adriatic Sea. Capture the magical moment with your camera or simply savour the beauty of nature's nightly spectacle.

Visit the Birth House of Vlaho Bukovac

Delve into the life of renowned Croatian painter Vlaho Bukovac by visiting his birth house, located in the heart of Cavtat's historic centre. Built in the 18th century, the stone house is where Bukovac spent his early years before embarking on a successful artistic career in Europe. Today, the house has been converted into a museum dedicated to Bukovac's life and work, featuring exhibits on his upbringing, education, and artistic achievements.

Stroll Along the Cavtat Promenade (Riva)

Take a leisurely stroll along the picturesque Cavtat Promenade (Riva), which stretches along the town's waterfront and offers stunning views of the Adriatic Sea. Lined with palm trees, outdoor cafes, and colourful fishing boats, the promenade is the perfect place to soak up the Mediterranean atmosphere and enjoy a relaxing seaside walk. Stop to admire the historic buildings that line the promenade, including the Church of St. Nicholas and the Church of Our Lady of the Snow.

Relax on Pasjaca Beach

Escape the crowds and unwind on the pristine shores of Pasjaca Beach, located just a short drive from Cavtat. Tucked away at the base of a dramatic limestone cliff, Pasjaca Beach is a hidden gem known for its crystal-clear waters, golden sands, and rugged natural beauty. Spend the day sunbathing, swimming, and snorkelling in the azure Adriatic Sea, or simply enjoy the peace and serenity of this secluded paradise.

Explore the Konavle Valley

Venture inland to the picturesque Konavle Valley, a fertile region known for its lush landscapes, traditional villages, and rich cultural heritage. Explore charming hamlets such as Gruda and Čilipi, where you can discover ancient stone houses, historic churches, and artisan workshops. Visit local farms and orchards to sample fresh produce such as figs, olives, and citrus fruits, or take part in traditional activities such as olive oil pressing and grape harvesting.

As you bid farewell to Cavtat, take with you cherished memories of its enchanting Old Town streets, breath-taking coastal landscapes, and delectable culinary delights. Whether you are exploring ancient ruins, cruising the azure waters of the Adriatic, or simply soaking in the sun on a tranquil beach, Cavtat offers a truly unforgettable travel experience that will linger in your heart long after you've returned home.

Memories to treasure: Bid adieu to Cavtat's enchanting charms

Concluding your journey through Cavtat, a picturesque coastal town in Croatia, prompts reflection on the memories woven and experiences cherished. Cavtat's enduring allure, from its historic Old Town to its serene waterfront, etches a lasting impression on visitors, beckoning them to immerse in its cultural tapestry and natural splendour. The hospitality of locals, the flavours of local cuisine, and the tranquillity of coastal vistas blend to leave a lingering essence that resonates long after bidding adieu to this captivating seaside gem.

Exploring Cavtat reveals narratives in every cobblestone street, each historic edifice, and the gentle lapping of waves. Carrying Cavtat's essence forward, may recollections of cultural richness, culinary delights, and scenic wonders continue to inspire and captivate, evoking the allure of this hidden treasure along Croatia's Dalmatian coast.

Whether recalling ancient echoes, savouring local flavours, or relishing sunset hues over the Adriatic Sea, Cavtat's parting sentiments compose a symphony of experiences that echo within, inviting a return to its embrace.

Rovinj: Venetian romance, coastal charms

Glimpses of Rovinj: Where beauty beckons adventurers

In the heart of the Istrian coast lies Rovinj, a town that dances between the whispers of history and the vibrant hues of modernity. Its streets, like threads of a tapestry, weave together tales of ancient seafaring traditions and contemporary artistic expressions. Rovinj's skyline, adorned by the graceful silhouette of the Church of St. Euphemia, stands as a sentinel overlooking the Adriatic, where the past and present converge in a harmonious symphony of culture and charm. This coastal gem beckons travellers to wander through its maze of alleys, where each corner reveals a new chapter in the town's story, inviting exploration and discovery amidst the salty breeze and the echoes of centuries past.

Rovinj's essence is a blend of old-world allure and modern allurements, where the scent of pine mingles with the aroma of freshly caught seafood, and the laughter of locals harmonizes with the hum of artistic inspiration. From the vibrant hues of the local markets to the tranquil beauty of its secluded coves, Rovinj offers a sensory journey that captivates the soul and ignites the imagination. Here, time seems to slow down, allowing visitors to savour each moment, whether indulging in culinary delights at seaside cafes, admiring the intricate details of historic architecture, or simply basking in the warmth of the Mediterranean sun along its rugged coastline.

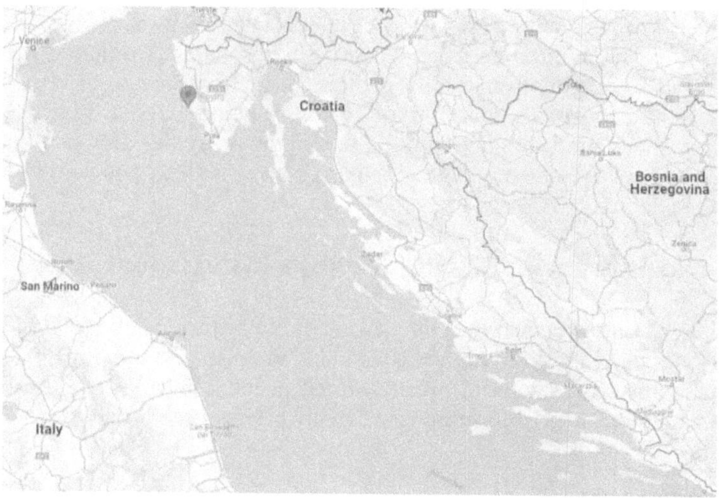

Legends of the sea: Rovinj's maritime heritage explored

Rovinj, with its rich historical tapestry, is a living testament to the crossroads of civilizations that have shaped its identity over the centuries. Tracing its origins back to ancient times when it was known as Ruginium, the town flourished under Roman rule, serving as an important port and centre of trade in the Adriatic. Through the centuries, Rovinj witnessed the ebb and flow of empires, including Byzantine, Venetian, and Austro-Hungarian influences, each leaving their indelible mark on its architecture, culture, and traditions.

One of the most iconic landmarks of Rovinj is the Church of St. Euphemia, perched atop a hill overlooking the town. Built in the 18th century in honour of the town's patron saint, the church's towering bell tower has become a symbol of Rovinj's skyline. Additionally, the narrow streets of the Old Town are lined with centuries-old buildings, elegant palaces, and charming squares, offering a glimpse into Rovinj's storied past. As visitors wander through its historic streets, they are transported back in time, where every cobblestone whispers tales of bygone eras and the resilience of a town shaped by history.

Embracing tradition: Rovinj's rich tapestry of life

Rovinj's local culture is a vibrant tapestry woven with threads of tradition, artistry, and community spirit. At its heart beats a deep reverence for the sea, as generations of Rovinj residents have relied on fishing and maritime trade for their livelihoods. Today, this seafaring heritage is celebrated through festivals, regattas, and the annual Feast of St. Lawrence, where locals pay homage to the patron saint of fishermen with colourful processions and maritime blessings.

Artistic expression also thrives in Rovinj, with the town serving as a haven for painters, sculptors, and artisans. The cobbled streets of the Old Town are lined with galleries and studios, showcasing the works of local talents inspired by the town's picturesque landscapes and rich cultural heritage. Music, too, resonates throughout Rovinj, with live performances ranging from traditional folk music to contemporary jazz filling the air during summer festivals and cultural events. Whether savouring the flavours of Istrian cuisine at a family-run tavern or joining in the festivities of a local celebration, visitors to Rovinj are welcomed with open arms into the heart and soul of its vibrant local culture.

Landmarks of legacy: Tracing Rovinj's historic footsteps

Explore the winding streets of the Old Town, admire historic landmarks, and discover hidden gems tucked away along the coastline. Whether you are strolling along the waterfront promenade, savouring fresh seafood in local tavernas, or soaking up the Mediterranean sun on pristine beaches, Rovinj offers a memorable experience for every visitor.

Punta Corrente park

Also known as Zlatni Rt (Golden Cape) Park, Punta Corrente is a verdant oasis located just a short walk from the Old Town. This protected nature reserve boasts lush Mediterranean vegetation, scenic walking trails, and secluded coves ideal for swimming and sunbathing. Explore the park's network of trails on foot or by bike, and discover hidden viewpoints offering breath-taking vistas of the coastline and surrounding islands.

Rovinj aquarium

Housed within the historic Batana House, the Rovinj Aquarium offers a fascinating glimpse into the marine life of the Adriatic Sea. Explore a variety of themed exhibits showcasing the diverse ecosystems and species found in the waters of Istria. From colourful reef fish to octopuses and sea turtles, the aquarium provides an educational and immersive experience for visitors of all ages, highlighting the importance of marine conservation in the region.

Grisia street

Known as Rovinj's 'artist street,' Grisia is a vibrant thoroughfare lined with galleries, studios, and artisan shops. Wander along its picturesque cobblestone lanes and browse a diverse array of artwork, including paintings, sculptures, and handmade crafts created by local artists.

Old town

Rovinj's Old Town is a maze of narrow cobblestone streets, adorned with colourful facades and centuries-old buildings. As you wander through its charming alleys, you'll encounter artisan workshops, cozy cafes, and boutique shops selling local crafts. Do not miss the chance to explore the Batana Eco-Museum, where you can learn about the traditional fishing boats of Rovinj, known as batanas, and the maritime heritage of the region.

Rovinj heritage museum

Housed within the imposing Baroque-style Baroque Palace, the Rovinj Heritage Museum offers a comprehensive overview of the town's rich cultural heritage. Explore its extensive collection of artifacts, archaeological finds, and historical exhibits, spanning the prehistoric, Roman, and medieval periods.

Monte Mulini forest park

Situated on the outskirts of Rovinj, Monte Mulini Forest Park is a scenic nature reserve encompassing lush woodland, meandering trails, and panoramic viewpoints. Take a leisurely stroll through the forest, immersing yourself in the tranquil surroundings and enjoying the fresh air. Keep an eye out for native flora and fauna, including pine trees, oak groves, and Mediterranean shrubs, as well as bird species such as woodpeckers and falcons.

Monkodonja archaeological site

Located just a short drive from Rovinj, the Monkodonja archaeological site offers a fascinating glimpse into Istria's prehistoric past. This Bronze Age hillfort dates back over 3,000 years and is characterized by its well-preserved defensive walls, dwellings, and artifacts.

Rovinj marina

Nestled along the waterfront, Rovinj Marina is a bustling hub for maritime activities and leisure pursuits. Stroll along its promenade lined with yachts and fishing boats, soaking up the maritime atmosphere and scenic views of the Adriatic Sea. Stop by one of the waterfront cafes or restaurants to savour fresh seafood dishes and watch the comings and goings of boats in the harbour.

Church of St. Euphemia

Perched atop a hill overlooking the town, the Church of St. Euphemia is an architectural masterpiece dedicated to the patron saint of Rovinj. The church's striking bell tower, modelled after the famous campanile in Venice, offers panoramic views of the Adriatic Sea and the surrounding islands.

Rovinj town clock

Perched atop a prominent hill overlooking the Old Town, the Rovinj Town Clock is a distinctive feature of the city's skyline. Dating back to the 12th century, the clock tower offers panoramic views of Rovinj's picturesque harbour, rooftops, and surrounding countryside. Visitors can climb to the top of the tower to enjoy breath-taking vistas and capture memorable photos of their time in Rovinj.

Lone bay

Tucked away on the southern coast of Rovinj, Lone Bay is a hidden gem known for its natural beauty and tranquil ambiance. This secluded cove boasts crystal-clear waters, pebbly beaches, and lush Mediterranean vegetation, making it an idyllic spot for swimming, sunbathing, and relaxation.

Batana house museum

Located in the heart of Rovinj's Old Town, the Batana House Museum offers insight into the traditional way of life of Rovinj's fishermen. Housed within a historic stone building, the museum showcases exhibit on the construction and use of batana boats, traditional fishing techniques, and the cultural heritage of Rovinj's fishing community.

Golden cape forest park

Stretching along the scenic coastline south of Rovinj, Golden Cape Forest Park is a vast natural reserve renowned for its pristine landscapes and diverse ecosystems. Visitors can explore the park's network of hiking and biking trails, which meander through fragrant pine forests, rocky coves, and secluded beaches. The Park also offers opportunities for birdwatching, picnicking, and enjoying panoramic views of the Adriatic Sea and surrounding islands.

Balbi's arch

Constructed in the 17th century by the Venetian architect Michele Sanmicheli, Balbi's Arch is a symbol of Rovinj's Venetian heritage. The imposing stone arch marks the entrance to the Old Town and serves as a gateway to the historic heart of the city. Admire its elegant design and decorative motifs, which reflect the architectural style of the Venetian Republic.

As the sun sets over Rovinj's enchanting skyline, take a moment to reflect on the timeless beauty and enduring charm of this coastal gem. Whether you've explored its historic landmarks, indulged in its culinary delights, or simply relaxed in its natural splendour, Rovinj leaves a lasting impression on all who visit. As you bid farewell to this captivating town, carry with you memories of its rich history, warm hospitality, and breath-taking landscapes, knowing that Rovinj will always hold a special place in your heart.

Culinary harmony: Delights along Rovinj's gastronomic pathway

As you wander through the cobblestone alleyways of this enchanting coastal town, you'll discover an abundance of culinary delights waiting to be savoured. From the earthy flavours of Istrian truffles to the fruity notes of extra virgin olive oil and the rich aromas of local wines and cheeses, Rovinj offers a gastronomic journey that reflects the region's diverse landscapes and cultural heritage. Join us as we explore the culinary treasures of Rovinj, where each dish tells a story of tradition, craftsmanship, and the bounty of the Adriatic Sea.

Rovinj scampi

Renowned for its succulent and flavourful taste, Rovinj scampi is a must-try delicacy for seafood lovers. These large Adriatic prawns are typically grilled, boiled, or sautéed with garlic, olive oil, and parsley, resulting in a dish that is both simple and divine. Savour the tender texture and sweet, briny flavour of these locally caught scampi at one of Rovinj's waterfront restaurants for an unforgettable dining experience.

Istrian prosciutto

Delight in the savoury goodness of Istrian prosciutto, a dry-cured ham that epitomizes the art of traditional charcuterie in the region. Made from locally raised pigs and seasoned with sea salt, pepper, and aromatic herbs, Istrian prosciutto is aged for several months to develop its distinctive flavour and tender texture. Enjoy thinly sliced prosciutto paired with creamy Istrian cheese, olives, and crusty bread for a classic Istrian appetizer that showcases the region's culinary expertise.

Istrian pasta

Dive into the world of Istrian pasta with a plate of fuži, a traditional pasta shape that is synonymous with Istrian cuisine. These hand-rolled pasta ribbons are typically served with a variety of sauces, from hearty meat ragu to creamy truffle sauce, showcasing the versatility of Istrian culinary traditions. Sample fuži at local trattorias and konobas in Rovinj for an authentic taste of Istria's pasta-making heritage.

Seafood risotto

Indulge in the rich and savoury flavours of seafood risotto, a beloved dish that highlights the bounty of the Adriatic Sea. Made with Arborio rice, fresh seafood such as shrimp, mussels, and calamari, and infused with white wine, garlic, and herbs, seafood risotto is a comforting and satisfying meal that is perfect for enjoying al fresco in Rovinj's charming Old Town.

Truffle pasta

Indulge in the earthy and aromatic flavours of Istrian truffles with a plate of truffle pasta in Rovinj. This regional specialty features homemade pasta, such as fuzi or pljukanci, tossed in a creamy sauce infused with black or white truffles. Garnished with grated truffle cheese and fresh herbs, this dish offers a decadent and satisfying culinary experience that highlights the unique terroir of Istria.

Truffle Delicacies

Delve into the world of truffle delicacies in Rovinj, where the prized Istrian white and black truffles take centre stage. From truffle-infused oils and cheeses to decadent truffle pastas and risottos, Rovinj offers a tantalizing array of dishes that celebrate the earthy flavours of these coveted fungi.

Artisanal Gelato

Treat yourself to a scoop of artisanal gelato in Rovinj, where gelaterias offer a tempting array of flavours made with fresh, locally sourced ingredients. Indulge in classics like creamy pistachio and decadent chocolate, or opt for inventive flavours inspired by Istrian ingredients such as fig, lavender, and honey.

Istrian Sausages

Experience the savoury delights of Istrian sausages, a staple of the region's culinary heritage that reflects its rustic charm and agricultural traditions. Made from a blend of pork, beef, and spices, Istrian sausages are typically seasoned with garlic, paprika, and herbs before being smoked or grilled to perfection.

Cheese Tastings

Delight in the flavours of artisanal cheeses produced in the rolling hills surrounding Rovinj, where local dairy farms craft an array of delicious cheeses from cow, sheep, and goat milk. Sample creamy cow's milk cheeses like Istrian Pag and Kozlar, tangy sheep's milk cheeses like Istrian Paski Sir and Dalmatian Paški Sir, and aromatic goat cheeses like Istrian Kiseli Sir and Dalmatian Skuta. Pair these delectable cheeses with fresh bread, honey, and Istrian wines for a memorable tasting experience.

Oysters and Mussels

Delight in the briny flavours of fresh oysters and mussels harvested from the pristine waters of the Adriatic Sea in Rovinj. Known for their plump and succulent texture, Istrian oysters and mussels are prized for their delicate flavour and are often enjoyed raw on the half-shell or served with a squeeze of lemon and a dash of vinegar. Pair these delectable shellfish with a glass of crisp white wine or sparkling prosecco for a quintessentially Istrian dining experience.

In conclusion, Rovinj offers a delectable array of culinary delights that celebrate the region's rich culinary heritage and natural bounty. From fresh seafood and truffle-infused pasta to locally produced olive oil and wine, there is something to tantalize every palate in this charming coastal town. Whether you are savouring the flavours of the sea, indulging in Istrian delicacies, or satisfying your sweet tooth with traditional desserts, Rovinj promises a memorable gastronomic journey that captures the essence of Istria's culinary traditions.

Enigmatic charms: Discovering Rovinj's best-kept secrets

Tucked away in the narrow streets and hidden corners of Rovinj lie treasures waiting to be discovered by intrepid travellers. These hidden gems offer glimpses into the town's rich history, vibrant culture, and stunning natural beauty. From secret viewpoints offering panoramic vistas of the Adriatic to tucked-away cafes serving up artisanal delicacies, Rovinj's hidden gems are as diverse as they are enchanting. Join us as we uncover some of the town's best-kept secrets and unlock the magic of Rovinj's hidden gems.

Zlatni Rt sculpture park

Located within the Golden Cape Forest Park, the Zlatni Rt Sculpture Park is a hidden gem that combines art and nature in a unique outdoor setting. The Park features a collection of contemporary sculptures created by Croatian and international artists, scattered throughout the forested landscape. Visitors can wander along meandering pathways, encountering sculptures that range from abstract forms to figurative works inspired by the natural world.

Rovinj wine trail

For wine enthusiasts seeking a unique experience off the beaten path, the Rovinj Wine Trail is a hidden gem waiting to be explored. This self-guided walking tour takes visitors through Rovinj's picturesque countryside, where they can discover hidden vineyards, family-owned wineries, and charming wine cellars tucked away in the hills. Along the way, visitors can sample a variety of local wines, including Istrian Malvasia, Teran, and Muscat, while learning about the region's winemaking traditions and tasting notes from knowledgeable vintners.

St. Thomas island

This small uninhabited island off the coast of Rovinj is a hidden gem for nature lovers and adventure seekers. Accessible by boat, St. Thomas Island boasts pristine beaches, crystal-clear waters, and scenic hiking trails that offer stunning views of the surrounding coastline.

Lim bay

Often referred to as the 'Adriatic fjord,' Lim Bay is a stunning natural wonder located just a short distance from Rovinj. This hidden gem is a long, narrow inlet flanked by steep limestone cliffs, with calm waters that are perfect for kayaking, boating, and swimming. Visitors can explore the bay's rich biodiversity, spotting rare bird species, marine life, and lush vegetation along its shores. For a truly unforgettable experience, sunset boat tours offer the chance to witness the bay's dramatic beauty in the golden light of dusk.

Dvigrad

Nestled in the Istrian countryside, Dvigrad is a hidden gem steeped in history and mystery. This abandoned medieval village offers visitors a glimpse into the region's past, with its crumbling stone walls, overgrown ruins, and ancient churches. Exploring Dvigrad feels like stepping back in time, as you wander through narrow alleyways and deserted courtyards, imagining the lives of the people who once called this place home.

Mon perin

Tucked away on the Istrian coast near Rovinj, Mon Perin is a hidden gem that offers a serene retreat from the hustle and bustle of city life. This picturesque village is surrounded by olive groves, vineyards, and rolling hills, with charming stone houses and narrow cobblestone streets that exude old-world charm. Visitors can explore the village's historic churches, traditional taverns, and artisan shops, or simply take a leisurely stroll through the countryside, soaking in the peaceful atmosphere and breathtaking views of the Adriatic Sea.

Sveta Eufemija peninsula

Situated just south of Rovinj's old town, the Sveta Eufemija Peninsula is a hidden gem that offers a tranquil escape from the crowds. This pristine natural reserve is home to secluded beaches, rocky coves, and fragrant pine forests, making it the perfect spot for a relaxing day by the sea. Visitors can swim in the crystal-clear waters, sunbathe on the pebbly shores, or explore the rugged coastline on foot.

Golden Cape Forest Park

Just a short walk from Rovinj's town centre lies the Golden Cape Forest Park, a hidden gem of natural beauty and tranquillity. This sprawling parkland encompasses lush Mediterranean vegetation, scenic walking and biking trails, and secluded coves perfect for swimming and sunbathing. Visitors can escape the crowds and immerse themselves in the peaceful ambiance of the forest, while enjoying panoramic views of the Adriatic Sea and nearby islands.

Valdibora market

For a taste of local life in Rovinj, head to the Valdibora Market, a hidden gem tucked away in the heart of the old town. Here, visitors can wander through stalls piled high with fresh produce, local delicacies, and handmade crafts, while soaking in the vibrant atmosphere of this bustling marketplace.

Discovering Rovinj's hidden gems is like unlocking a treasure trove of unforgettable experiences. Whether you are wandering down ancient alleyways, exploring historic landmarks, or immersing yourself in nature, each hidden gem offers a glimpse into the soul of this enchanting coastal town. As you bid farewell to Rovinj, carry with you the memories of these hidden treasures, knowing that the magic of discovery awaits around every corner.

Nature's wonderland: Exploring Rovinj's outdoor marvels

Nestled on Croatia's Istrian Peninsula, Rovinj boasts a stunning natural landscape that beckons outdoor enthusiasts from around the world. From rugged coastline to verdant forests, this picturesque town offers a myriad of outdoor activities for visitors to enjoy. Whether you are seeking adventure on land or sea, Rovinj has something for everyone to explore and discover.

Sea kayaking
Explore Rovinj's rugged coastline and hidden coves on a sea kayaking adventure.

Paddle through crystal-clear waters, past rocky cliffs, and under natural arches while taking in panoramic views of the Adriatic Sea. Guided tours are available for all skill levels, allowing you to discover secluded beaches and marine wildlife along the way.

Cycling

Hit the trails and explore Rovinj's picturesque countryside by bike. With a network of cycling paths winding through olive groves, vineyards, and coastal villages, cycling is a fantastic way to experience the region's natural beauty up close. Rent a bike or join a guided cycling tour to discover charming hilltop towns, historic sites, and breath-taking viewpoints.

Snorkelling and scuba diving

Dive into Rovinj's underwater world and discover a vibrant marine ecosystem teeming with colourful fish, coral reefs, and fascinating sea creatures. Snorkelling and scuba diving sites abound along the coastline, offering clear visibility and diverse marine life.

Rock climbing

Test your skills on Rovinj's rugged cliffs and limestone crags with a rock-climbing excursion. The region boasts numerous climbing routes suitable for climbers of all levels, from beginners to seasoned professionals. Enjoy panoramic views of the Adriatic Sea as you scale vertical walls and conquer challenging routes under the guidance of experienced instructors.

Sailing and boat tours

Set sail on the Adriatic Sea and explore Rovinj's stunning coastline aboard a sailing yacht or traditional wooden boat. Join a guided boat tour to visit nearby islands, secluded beaches, and coastal landmarks, or charter a private boat for a personalized adventure.

Hiking

Lace up your hiking boots and explore Rovinj's scenic trails that wind through lush forests, rolling hills, and coastal cliffs. Choose from a variety of hiking routes, ranging from easy walks suitable for families to challenging treks for experienced hikers. Along the way, you'll encounter stunning viewpoints, hidden waterfalls, and ancient ruins, providing opportunities to immerse yourself in the region's natural and cultural heritage.

Stand-up paddleboarding

Experience Rovinj's coastline from a different perspective as you glide across the water on a stand-up paddleboard. Whether you are a beginner or an experienced paddler, SUP offers a fun and relaxing way to explore the shoreline, discover hidden caves and secluded beaches, and soak up the sun.

Fishing excursions

Embark on a fishing adventure in the waters surrounding Rovinj and try your hand at catching a variety of fish species that inhabit the Adriatic Sea. Join a guided fishing excursion led by experienced local fishermen who will share their knowledge of the best fishing spots and techniques.

Birdwatching

Rovinj's diverse natural habitats provide an ideal setting for birdwatching enthusiasts to observe a wide variety of bird species in their natural environment. From coastal wetlands and salt marshes to forests and meadows, the region is home to an array of birdlife, including herons, flamingos, eagles, and migratory birds. Bring your binoculars and camera and explore designated birdwatching areas to spot these feathered inhabitants.

Zip-lining

Soar through the treetops and experience an adrenaline rush on a zip-lining adventure in Rovinj's scenic countryside. Zip-line courses offer thrilling rides over forests, valleys, and canyons, providing panoramic views of the landscape below. Suitable for adventurers of all ages, zip-lining is a memorable way to experience the beauty of Rovinj's natural surroundings and add a dash of excitement to your vacation.

Picnicking

Escape the hustle and bustle of the town and enjoy a leisurely picnic amidst the natural beauty of Rovinj's parks, forests, and coastal areas. Pack a basket with local delicacies, fresh produce, and refreshing beverages, then find a scenic spot to spread out a blanket and savour a delicious meal surrounded by breath-taking scenery.

With its stunning coastline, scenic countryside, and wealth of outdoor activities, Rovinj offers endless opportunities for adventure and exploration. Whether you are kayaking along the coast, cycling through vineyards, or diving beneath the waves, the natural beauty of Rovinj provides the perfect backdrop for outdoor enthusiasts to immerse themselves in nature and create unforgettable memories.

Tradition in bloom: Rovinj's vibrant festival scene

Rovinj Summer Festival (Rovinj Ljetna Noć): This vibrant summer festival celebrates the rich cultural heritage of Rovinj with a diverse program of events including concerts, theatre performances, art exhibitions, and street parades. Held throughout the summer months, the Rovinj Summer Festival showcases local and international talent, attracting visitors from near and far to experience the lively atmosphere and artistic creativity that fills the streets of the Old Town.

Festa di San Eufemia (September)

Celebrated annually on September 16th, St. Euphemia's Feast Day honours the patron saint of Rovinj with religious ceremonies, processions, and festivities. The highlight of the celebration is the solemn mass held at the Church of St. Euphemia, followed by a lively procession through the streets of the Old Town. Visitors can join in the festivities, enjoying traditional music, dance, and local delicacies as they pay homage to the beloved saint.

Rovinjski Karneval (February/March)

The Rovinj Carnival is a festive celebration held in the weeks leading up to Lent, with colourful parades, costume contests, and street parties taking place throughout the town. Participants don elaborate costumes and masks, joining in the lively processions that wind their way through the streets, accompanied by music, dancing, and revelry. The Rovinj Carnival is a time-honoured tradition that brings together locals and visitors alike to celebrate joyfully before the solemn period of Lent begins.

Rovinjski Art Kolin (July)

This annual art event brings together talented artists from Croatia and beyond to create and exhibit their work in the picturesque setting of Rovinj. Held during the summer months, the Rovinj Art Colony features plein air painting sessions, workshops, and exhibitions, allowing visitors to observe artists at work and purchase original artworks directly from the creators. The colony's diverse program includes a variety of artistic styles and mediums, reflecting the vibrant creative spirit of Rovinj's cultural scene.

Dan Grada Rovinja (September)

Held in September, Rovinj Heritage Day is dedicated to preserving and promoting the town's rich cultural heritage. The event features guided tours of historic landmarks, open-air exhibitions, and traditional craft demonstrations, providing visitors with insight into Rovinj's fascinating history and architectural treasures. Local artisans showcase their skills in pottery, lace-making, and other traditional crafts, offering visitors the chance to purchase unique souvenirs and support the local community.

Noć Batane (July/August)

This annual event pays tribute to Rovinj's maritime heritage and the traditional wooden boats known as batanas that have long been used by local fishermen. Held in late summer, Rovinj Batana Night features a colourful parade of illuminated batanas sailing through the harbour, accompanied by live music, dance performances, and fireworks. Visitors can sample freshly caught seafood, participate in boat races, and learn about the important role that batanas have played in Rovinj's cultural identity.

Rovinjsko Proljeće (April)

As the winter chill gives way to warmer weather, Rovinj comes alive with the sights and sounds of spring during the Rovinj Spring Festival. Held in April, this vibrant event celebrates the season of renewal with outdoor concerts, art exhibitions, and culinary delights. Visitors can stroll through colourful flower markets, sample local wines and olive oils, and enjoy al fresco dining in the town's charming squares and waterfront promenades.

Rovinj International Salsa Festival (June)

Salsa enthusiasts from around the world converge on Rovinj every summer for the Rovinj International Salsa Festival, one of the largest salsa events in Europe. Over several days in June, the town pulsates with the infectious rhythms of Latin music as participants attend workshops, performances, and social dances led by world-class instructors and DJs. Whether you are a seasoned dancer or a beginner, the festival offers a vibrant and inclusive atmosphere where you can learn new moves, make friends, and immerse yourself in the joy of salsa.

Rovinjski Ribarski Festival (August)

Celebrating Rovinj's rich fishing heritage, the Fishermen's Festival takes place in August, offering visitors a taste of traditional Istrian seafood dishes and culinary delights. Local fishermen showcase their catch of the day, including freshly grilled fish, octopus salad, and squid ink risotto, while stalls line the waterfront selling seafood specialties and homemade wine. Live music, dancing, and cultural performances add to the festive ambiance, making it a must-visit event for food enthusiasts and culture seekers alike.

Međunarodni Filmski Festival Rovinj (October)

Film buffs flock to Rovinj in October for the International Film Festival, a showcase of independent and international cinema. The festival screens a diverse selection of feature films, documentaries, and shorts from around the world, with screenings held in various venues across the town. In addition to film screenings, the festival hosts panel discussions, workshops, and networking events, providing filmmakers and cinephiles with opportunities to connect and engage with the global film community.

Unlocking Rovinj's charms: Insider tips for travellers

With its charming cobblestone streets, historic architecture, and stunning seaside setting, Rovinj is a beloved destination for travellers seeking beauty, culture, and relaxation. Whether you are wandering through the Old Town's narrow alleys, soaking up the sun on pristine beaches, or savouring fresh seafood in waterfront restaurants, Rovinj offers a wealth of experiences waiting to be discovered. To make the most of your visit, here are some travel tips to enhance your Rovinj experience.

Explore the Old Town

Lose yourself in the labyrinthine streets of Rovinj's Old Town, where centuries-old buildings, colourful facades, and Venetian influences create an enchanting atmosphere. Wander through the winding alleyways, browse boutique shops, and admire historic landmarks like the Church of St. Euphemia, whose towering bell tower offers panoramic views of the town and surrounding islands.

Sunset Sailing

Experience the magic of Rovinj's coastline by embarking on a sunset sailing tour. Cruise along the Adriatic Sea aboard a traditional wooden boat and watch as the sun dips below the horizon, casting golden hues over the water and illuminating the town's iconic skyline.

Climb to St. Euphemia's Bell Tower

For panoramic vistas of Rovinj and its surroundings, climb the 60-meter-high bell tower of the Church of St. Euphemia. Ascend the narrow staircase to the top, where you'll be rewarded with sweeping views of the Old Town, harbour, and nearby islands. Visit during the early morning or late afternoon to avoid crowds and enjoy the serene beauty of Rovinj from above.

Cycling Adventure in Golden Cape Park

Explore the natural beauty of Rovinj's Golden Cape Park (Zlatni Rt) by embarking on a cycling adventure. Rent a bike and follow scenic trails that wind through pine forests, along rugged coastline, and past hidden beaches. Stop to admire panoramic viewpoints, take a refreshing swim in secluded coves, and enjoy a picnic amidst the tranquillity of nature.

Local Artisan Workshops

Immerse yourself in Rovinj's vibrant arts scene by visiting local artisan workshops scattered throughout the Old Town. Discover traditional crafts such as ceramics, jewellery-making, and lacework, and observe skilled artisans at work in their studios.

Explore the Lim Fjord by Kayak

Experience the natural beauty of the Lim Fjord, a stunning coastal inlet located just south of Rovinj, by embarking on a kayaking adventure. Paddle through crystal-clear waters flanked by lush greenery and towering cliffs, and discover hidden caves and secluded beaches along the fjord's winding coastline. With local guides leading the way, you'll learn about the area's rich biodiversity and geological significance while enjoying a memorable day on the water.

Attend a Fisherman's Feast

Dive into Rovinj's maritime heritage by attending a traditional fisherman's feast, known locally as a 'ribarska fešta.' These lively events celebrate the town's fishing culture and culinary traditions, with fresh seafood dishes served up alongside live music, dancing, and entertainment. Join locals and visitors alike in indulging in an array of freshly caught seafood specialties, from grilled fish to octopus salad, while soaking up the festive atmosphere under the stars.

Relax on Lone Bay Beach

Escape the hustle and bustle of the town centre and unwind on the pristine shores of Lone Bay Beach. Located just a short walk or bike ride from Rovinj's Old Town, this tranquil oasis offers soft pebble beaches, clear turquoise waters, and lush pine forests providing shade from the sun. Spend a leisurely day swimming, sunbathing, or simply soaking in the natural beauty of this idyllic coastal setting.

Explore the Islands

Embark on a boat tour to explore the nearby islands of Rovinj, such as St. Andrew's Island and St. Catherine's Island. Discover secluded coves, hidden beaches, and ancient ruins as you island-hop across the sparkling Adriatic Sea. Opt for a guided tour to learn about the islands' history, flora, and fauna, or rent a kayak or paddleboard to explore at your own pace.

Discover Rovinj's Street Art

Wander off the beaten path to uncover Rovinj's vibrant street art scene, with colourful murals and graffiti adorning alleyways and building facades throughout the town. Join a guided street art tour or simply wander at your own pace to discover hidden gems created by local and international artists. From whimsical designs to thought-provoking pieces, Rovinj's street art adds a contemporary flair to its historic streets.

Reflections on paradise: Rovinj's beauty lingers in memory

Concluding your journey through Rovinj, a town that embodies a harmonious blend of history, culture, and natural splendour, leaves you with a tapestry of memories woven with the threads of ancient charm and modern allure. Rovinj's picturesque streets, adorned with colourful facades and steeped in maritime heritage, resonate with the echoes of centuries past, inviting you to immerse yourself in its rich tapestry of traditions and scenic beauty. The town's iconic landmarks, from the elegant Church of St. Euphemia to the bustling harbour, stand as testaments to its enduring allure, while the vibrant arts scene and culinary delights add a contemporary flair to this coastal gem on the Adriatic coast.

As you bid farewell to Rovinj, the essence of the town lingers in your heart, a melange of historic echoes, artistic inspirations, and coastal vistas that have left an indelible mark on your soul. The warmth of the locals, the flavours of local cuisine, and the serenity of the coastal landscapes have combined to create a symphony of experiences that resonate within, evoking a sense of gratitude and wonder for the beauty and magic found in this captivating seaside town. Rovinj's closing thoughts are a testament to the enduring allure of a destination where the past and present intertwine, inviting you to carry the spirit of Rovinj with you as you venture forth, enriched by the memories of your time spent in this coastal haven.

Skradin-Tranquil haven, forested delights

Riverside reverie: Exploring hidden gems in Dalmatian splendour

Skradin, a town nestled in the heart of the Krka National Park, is a place where history and nature converge in a harmonious embrace. A hidden gem along the Dalmatian coast of Croatia, Skradin's charm lies in its ability to captivate visitors with its rich cultural heritage and the breath-taking beauty of its surroundings. The town's ancient roots, dating back to the Roman era, are evident in its well-preserved architecture, narrow cobblestone streets, and the remnants of its medieval walls. Skradin's location at the mouth of the Krka River, surrounded by lush forests and cascading waterfalls, adds to its allure, inviting travellers to embark on a journey of discovery that encompasses the best of both history and nature.

Skradin's unique blend of ancient and natural wonders creates a destination that appeals to history buffs, nature lovers, and food enthusiasts alike. The town's warm Mediterranean climate, crystal-clear waters, and delectable cuisine further enhance its appeal, making Skradin a destination that promises a harmonious fusion of tradition and modernity against the backdrop of the Krka River. Whether exploring the historic Old Town, indulging in local delicacies at charming cafes, or embarking on a boat tour to witness the majesty of the Krka waterfalls, Skradin offers a journey filled with cultural immersion, scenic wonders, and moments of serenity along the Dalmatian coast.

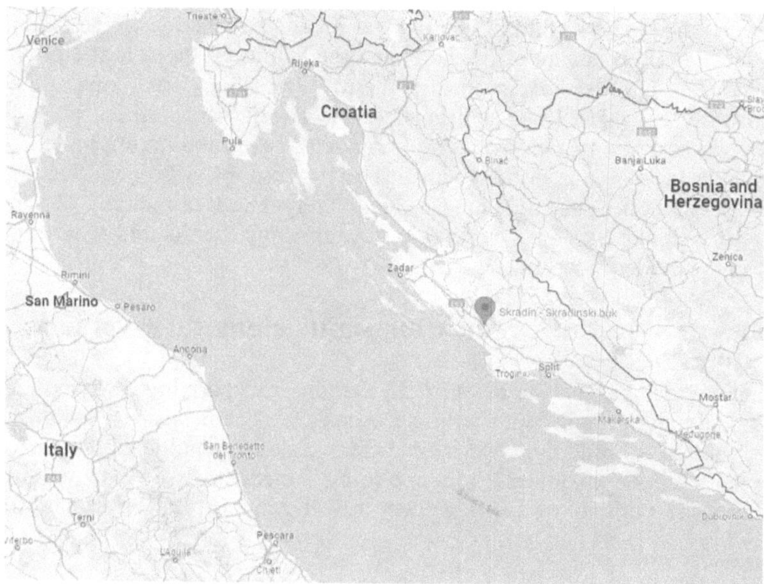

River echoes: Skradin's historic waterfront unveiled

Skradin's historical significance is deeply intertwined with its strategic location along the Adriatic coast and the Krka River. Dating back to ancient times, Skradin served as an important settlement for the Illyrians, who recognized the strategic importance of its position at the head of the Krka estuary. In the Roman era, Skradin, known as Scardona, flourished as a bustling port and a key hub for trade and commerce in the region. The Romans recognized the natural beauty and strategic value of the area, and remnants of their presence, including ancient city walls and archaeological sites, still dot the landscape today.

Throughout the centuries, Skradin has been shaped by various cultures and civilizations, including the Byzantines, Venetians, and Ottomans, each leaving their mark on the town's architecture, culture, and traditions. The Venetians, in particular, played a significant role in Skradin's history, establishing it as a fortified town and constructing the impressive fortress of Turina, which still stands sentinel over the town today. As visitors wander the streets of Skradin's charming Old Town, they are immersed in a living tapestry of history, where each cobblestone whispers tales of bygone eras and the resilience of a town shaped by centuries of influence and legacy.

Soul of Dalmatia: Celebrating Skradin's cultural mosaic

In Skradin, local culture thrives as a vibrant tapestry woven from centuries of tradition and community spirit. Here, amidst the rugged beauty of the Dalmatian coast, residents celebrate their heritage with pride, preserving age-old customs that have been passed down through generations. From lively folk festivals to intimate gatherings in family-run taverns, Skradin offers visitors a glimpse into the heart and soul of Croatian culture.

At the heart of Skradin's cultural identity lies a deep connection to the land and sea. Fishing has long been a way of life here, and the bounty of the Adriatic provides not only sustenance but also inspiration for the town's culinary traditions. Visitors can sample freshly caught seafood delicacies at local restaurants, where each dish is a testament to the region's rich maritime heritage. Beyond the dining table, Skradin's cultural landscape is also dotted with artisan workshops, where skilled craftsmen practice age-old trades such as stone carving, pottery, and lace-making. These artisans are the custodians of Skradin's cultural legacy, ensuring that its traditions continue to flourish in the modern world.

Wonders of Skradin: Captivating sights along the riverside

Nestled along the banks of the Krka River, Skradin is a charming town in the heart of Croatia's Dalmatia region. With its picturesque Old Town, historic landmarks, and stunning natural surroundings, Skradin offers visitors a unique blend of cultural heritage and outdoor adventure. From exploring ancient streets to discovering hidden gems, there is something to captivate every traveller in this idyllic destination.

Skradin old town

Skradin's Old Town is a captivating labyrinth of narrow cobblestone streets, adorned with historic buildings and traditional stone houses. Wander through its charming alleys to discover hidden squares, ancient churches, and local artisan shops. The Old Town's well-preserved architecture reflects centuries of history, offering a glimpse into Skradin's rich cultural heritage.

Skradin waterfront

The Skradin waterfront is a bustling hub of activity, where locals and tourists alike gather to enjoy the beauty of the Krka River. Quaint cafes, charming restaurants, and artisanal boutiques line the promenade, inviting visitors to relax and soak in the tranquil ambiance. From here, you can embark on boat tours to nearby attractions such as Krka National Park or simply savour the scenic views with a leisurely stroll.

Skradin city museum

Housed in a historic building in the town centre, the Skradin City Museum offers a fascinating journey through Skradin's past. Exhibits showcase archaeological treasures, artifacts from Roman and medieval times, and cultural relics that illuminate the town's heritage. From ancient pottery to medieval weaponry, the museum's collections provide valuable insights into Skradin's role as a crossroads of civilizations.

Visovac island

Situated in the middle of the Krka River, Visovac Island is a serene oasis of natural beauty and spiritual significance. Home to a Franciscan monastery dating back to the 15th century, the island exudes tranquillity and offers breath-taking views of its lush surroundings. Visitors can explore the monastery's museum, stroll through its peaceful gardens, and bask in the serenity of this idyllic retreat.

Medieval fortress of Turina

Perched atop a hill overlooking Skradin, the Medieval Fortress of Turina stands as a testament to Skradin's strategic importance throughout history. Dating back to the 14th century, the fortress offers panoramic views of the town and the Krka River below. Visitors can explore its ancient walls, towers, and courtyards, imagining the battles and sieges that once took place within its formidable walls.

Church of St. Barbara

Tucked away in the heart of Skradin's Old Town, the Church of St. Barbara is a hidden gem of medieval architecture and religious devotion. Built in the 15th century, the church is dedicated to St. Barbara, the patron saint of miners and artillerymen. Its interior features exquisite frescoes, intricate woodcarvings, and a peaceful ambiance that invites quiet contemplation.

Skradin wineries

Surrounding Skradin's picturesque hills are several acclaimed wineries renowned for their production of fine wines. Visitors can embark on wine tasting tours to sample a variety of local varietals, including the famous Babic red wine and Debit white wine. Learn about the winemaking process, savour the flavours of the region, and toast to the beauty of Skradin's vineyard-dotted landscape.

Roski slap waterfalls

Located within Krka National Park, the Roski Slap Waterfalls are a series of cascading waterfalls surrounded by lush greenery and scenic viewpoints. Visitors can hike along wooden walkways and admire the stunning beauty of the waterfalls, which flow into the Visovac Lake below. The tranquil ambiance and natural splendour make it a perfect spot for relaxation and photography.

Krka national park

Just a short boat ride from Skradin lies Krka National Park, a pristine wilderness teeming with natural wonders. From cascading waterfalls and emerald pools to verdant forests and limestone canyons, the park's diverse landscapes are a paradise for outdoor enthusiasts. Visitors can hike along scenic trails, swim beneath the waterfalls, or take a boat tour to explore the park's hidden corners.

St. Jacob's church

Overlooking the town of Skradin, St. Jacob's Church is a prominent landmark with its distinctive bell tower and Baroque architecture. Dating back to the 18th century, the church is dedicated to St. James the Greater and features ornate interior decorations, including altars, paintings, and sculptures. Visitors can admire the church's architectural details and enjoy panoramic views of the surrounding landscape from its vantage point.

Skradin bread factory

For a taste of authentic Croatian cuisine, be sure to visit the Skradin Bread Factory, where traditional Dalmatian bread is baked fresh daily. Using time-honoured recipes and locally sourced ingredients, the bakery produces a variety of breads, pastries, and sweet treats that are beloved by locals and visitors alike. Take a guided tour of the bakery to learn about the bread-making process and sample freshly baked delights straight from the oven.

Ethno village

Step back in time and experience rural Croatian life at the Ethno Village near Skradin. Set amidst rolling hills and vineyards, the village is a living museum showcasing traditional Dalmatian architecture, crafts, and customs. Visitors can explore rustic stone houses, watch artisans at work, and participate in hands-on activities such as pottery making and weaving. Immerse yourself in the rich cultural heritage of the region and gain insight into the timeless traditions of rural Croatia.

Skradin bridge

Spanning the Krka River, the Skradin Bridge is an architectural marvel dating back to the 19th century. Its elegant design and sturdy construction make it both a practical thoroughfare and a scenic viewpoint. As you traverse the bridge, you'll be treated to panoramic vistas of the river below, the bustling marina, and the verdant hills surrounding Skradin.

As the sun sets over the Krka River, casting a golden glow upon Skradin's historic streets and waterfront, you'll be left with memories to last a lifetime. Whether you've marvelled at the architecture of St. Spiridon's Church, crossed the iconic Skradin Bridge, or simply savoured the tranquillity of this charming town, Skradin leaves an indelible impression on all who visit. Plan your next adventure to Skradin and experience the magic of this hidden gem for yourself.

Gastronomic gems: A feast for the senses in Skradin

Welcome to Skradin, a hidden gem nestled in the heart of Dalmatia, where culinary delights await at every turn. From fresh seafood caught in the pristine waters of the Adriatic Sea to hearty stews simmered with local herbs and spices, Skradin offers a gastronomic adventure that tantalizes the taste buds and delights the senses. Join us as we explore the flavours of Skradin and uncover the culinary treasures that make this coastal town a food lover's paradise.

Skradin risotto

This traditional dish is a culinary masterpiece that perfectly captures the essence of Skradin. Made with locally sourced ingredients such as tender veal, flavourful mushrooms, and aromatic herbs, Skradin Risotto is slow-cooked to perfection in a rich broth made from veal bones and white wine. The result is a creamy and indulgent risotto that is bursting with savoury flavours and served as a hearty main course in many

Skradin cake

No visit to Skradin is complete without indulging in a slice of Skradin Cake, a decadent dessert that showcases the region's culinary expertise. This luscious cake features layers of delicate sponge cake soaked in a sweet syrup made from local liqueurs such as maraschino or amaretto. Sandwiched between the layers is a rich custard filling infused with citrus zest and topped with a velvety chocolate ganache.

Skradin bread

Skradin Bread is a traditional bread recipe that has been passed down through generations in the region. Made with simple ingredients such as flour, water, yeast, and salt, this rustic bread is characterized by its crusty exterior and soft, airy interior. Skradin Bread is typically baked in wood-fired ovens, imparting a delightful smoky flavour to the finished loaf.

Stuffed bell peppers

Punjene Paprike is a classic Croatian dish that is often served during special occasions and family gatherings in Skradin. Bell peppers are stuffed with a savoury mixture of ground meat, rice, onions, and spices, then simmered in a rich tomato sauce until tender and flavourful. The dish is hearty, comforting, and bursting with the robust flavours of the Mediterranean, making it a favourite among locals and visitors alike.

Fig delights

Figs are a beloved fruit in the Mediterranean, and Skradin's warm climate provides the perfect conditions for fig cultivation. Visitors can indulge in a variety of fig-infused treats, including fig jams, preserves, and desserts. Whether enjoyed on their own or incorporated into pastries and cakes, the sweet and luscious flavour of figs is a true delight for the taste buds.

Traditional Rakija tasting

Rakija, a fruit brandy popular throughout the Balkans, holds a special place in Croatian culture, and Skradin offers visitors the opportunity to sample a variety of traditional rakija. Made from locally sourced fruits such as grapes, plums, and cherries, each rakija boasts its own distinct flavour and character.

Maraschino liqueur

Skradin is famous for producing Maraschino liqueur, a sweet and aromatic cherry liqueur made from Marasca cherries. Dating back to the 16th century, this unique liqueur is still crafted using traditional methods, resulting in a smooth and flavourful drink with hints of almond and cherry.

Stuffed calamari

Fresh calamari are a staple of Croatian coastal cuisine, and in Skradin, it is often prepared in a unique and delicious way. Stuffed with a savoury mixture of breadcrumbs, garlic, parsley, and local spices, then grilled to perfection, stuffed calamari is a mouth-watering dish that showcases the fresh flavours of the Adriatic Sea.

Trout from the Krka River

Skradin is situated near the pristine waters of the Krka River, home to an abundance of freshwater fish, including trout. Grilled or roasted and served with a squeeze of lemon and a sprinkle of herbs, Krka River trout is a simple yet exquisite dish that allows the natural flavours of the fish to shine. Enjoyed alongside locally grown vegetables and a glass of Croatian wine, it is a true taste of Skradin's culinary delights.

Stuffed squid

Stuffed squid is a classic Dalmatian dish that showcases the region's love for seafood and simple yet flavourful cooking. Tender squid tubes are filled with a mixture of breadcrumbs, garlic, parsley, and sometimes rice or cheese, then gently simmered in a tomato-based sauce until tender. Served with a side of boiled potatoes or crusty bread, stuffed squid is a satisfying and homey meal that highlights the freshness of the ingredients.

Crostoli

Crostoli are delicate fried pastries that are popular throughout Croatia, especially during festive occasions. In Skradin, these crispy treats are often enjoyed during Carnival season or as part of holiday celebrations. Made from a simple dough that is rolled thin, cut into ribbons, and fried until golden and crispy, crostoli are dusted with powdered sugar for a touch of sweetness.

As you bid farewell to Skradin, take with you the memories of its culinary delights and the warmth of its hospitality. Whether you've indulged in Skradin risotto, savoured Dalmatian prosciutto, or sampled the town's famous olive oils, the flavours of Skradin will linger in your memory long after you've departed. As you continue your culinary journey, may the tastes and aromas of Skradin inspire you to savour every moment and embrace the rich tapestry of flavours that the world has to offer.

Mysteries revealed: Delving into Skradin's hidden delights

Welcome to Skradin, a charming town nestled on the banks of the Krka River in the heart of Croatia's Dalmatian coast. While Skradin is renowned for its stunning natural beauty and rich cultural heritage, it also boasts a treasure trove of hidden gems waiting to be explored. From secluded islands and cascading waterfalls to ancient ruins and sacred monasteries, these hidden gems offer a glimpse into Skradin's lesser-known wonders, inviting visitors to embark on a journey of discovery and adventure.

Roski slap waterfall

Away from the main tourist trails, Roski Slap Waterfall is a hidden gem that captivates with its raw beauty and untamed wilderness. Situated along the Krka River, the waterfall plunges into a series of cascades surrounded by lush greenery and dramatic cliffs.

Krka monastery

Located near the Krka River, the Krka Monastery is a hidden gem steeped in centuries of religious history and cultural significance. Founded in the 14th century, the monastery is known for its striking Byzantine-style architecture, picturesque setting, and valuable collection of religious artifacts. Visitors can explore the monastery's church, admire its frescoes and icons, and soak in the peaceful atmosphere of this hidden sanctuary.

Sibenik old town

Just a short distance from Skradin lies the picturesque old town of Sibenik, a hidden gem that transports visitors back in time with its medieval charm and historic landmarks. Wander through narrow cobblestone streets lined with stone houses, visit the imposing St. James's Cathedral, a UNESCO World Heritage Site, and soak in the atmosphere of centuries past in the town's charming squares and bustling markets.

Sokolarski Raptor centre

For nature enthusiasts and bird lovers, the Sokolarski Raptor Centre offers a unique opportunity to get up close and personal with some of Croatia's most majestic birds of prey. Located near Skradin, the centre is dedicated to the conservation and rehabilitation of endangered raptor species and offers guided tours and educational programs where visitors can learn about these magnificent creatures and witness breath-taking flight demonstrations.

Krka River canyon

Explore the rugged beauty of the Krka River Canyon, a hidden gem that offers stunning panoramic views and unparalleled opportunities for outdoor adventure. Hike along scenic trails that wind through the canyon's rocky cliffs and dense forests, marvel at the crystal-clear waters of the river below, and discover hidden caves and waterfalls tucked away amidst the pristine wilderness of this natural wonder.

Burnum Roman military camp

Tucked away amidst the rugged landscapes of the Krka National Park, Burnum Roman Military Camp is a hidden gem that offers a glimpse into Croatia's ancient history. Built by the Romans in the 1st century AD, the camp served as a strategic military outpost and features well-preserved ruins, including an amphitheatre and barracks. Visitors can explore the archaeological site, marvel at the ancient architecture, and imagine life in Roman times while enjoying the tranquillity of the surrounding countryside.

Skradin marina

Embark on a scenic boat tour of the Krka River and surrounding islands from the picturesque Skradin Marina, a hidden gem nestled in the heart of the town. Cruise along the tranquil waters, passing by secluded coves, hidden beaches, and ancient ruins, and soak in the breath-taking views of the Dalmatian coast from the comfort of your boat.

Bribirska Glavica archaeological site

Delve into Croatia's rich history at the Bribirska Glavica Archaeological Site, a hidden gem located near Skradin that offers a fascinating glimpse into the region's ancient past. This hilltop settlement dates back to the Illyrian and Roman periods and features well-preserved ruins, including ancient fortifications, tombs, and residential buildings.

Skradin's hidden water springs

Venture off the beaten path to uncover Skradin's hidden water springs, a natural wonder hidden away in the town's lush surroundings. Follow meandering trails through dense forests and along crystal-clear streams to discover secluded springs where you can cool off with a refreshing swim in pristine waters.

Sunset views from Skradin bridge

Experience the magic of a Dalmatian sunset from the iconic Skradin Bridge, a hidden gem that offers panoramic views of the town and surrounding landscape. As the sun dips below the horizon, casting golden hues across the sky, soak in the breath-taking beauty of the Krka River and distant mountains. This hidden vantage point provides a serene and unforgettable setting to witness nature's nightly spectacle and create lasting memories of your visit to Skradin.

Skradinski Buk waterfall

Tucked away in the depths of the Krka National Park, Skradinski Buk Waterfall is a hidden paradise waiting to be discovered. Cascading over a series of limestone terraces, the waterfall forms a series of natural pools ideal for swimming and relaxation. Surrounded by dense forests and rich biodiversity, Skradinski Buk offers visitors the chance to reconnect with nature and experience the timeless beauty of Croatia's natural wonders.

As you explore the hidden gems of Skradin, you'll uncover a world of beauty, history, and tranquillity that will leave a lasting impression on your heart and soul. From the serene shores of Visovac Island to the majestic cascades of Skradinski Buk Waterfall, each hidden gem offers a unique and unforgettable experience that will enrich your journey through this enchanting corner of Croatia. Embrace the spirit of exploration and allow yourself to be captivated by the hidden treasures of Skradin, where every discovery promises a new adventure and a deeper connection to the natural wonders of the Dalmatian coast.

Wilderness wanderlust: Outdoor adventures in Skradin's realm

Nestled along the banks of the Krka River, Skradin offers an abundance of outdoor activities for nature lovers and adventure seekers alike. From exploring the natural wonders of Krka National Park to kayaking on the pristine waters of the Krka River, there is no shortage of ways to immerse yourself in the stunning surroundings. Whether you prefer hiking through lush forests, cycling along scenic trails, or embarking on sailing adventures, Skradin provides the perfect base for outdoor enthusiasts to explore the diverse landscapes of Dalmatia.

Kayaking on the Krka River

Discover the beauty of the Krka River from a unique perspective with a kayaking excursion. Paddle through crystal-clear waters, navigate narrow channels, and explore hidden coves as you soak in the stunning natural scenery. Keep an eye out for native wildlife, including herons, otters, and even the occasional dolphin.

Cycling adventures

Rent a bike and set off on a cycling adventure through the picturesque countryside surrounding Skradin. Pedal along winding roads lined with olive groves and vineyards, passing through charming villages and ancient ruins along the way. With varying terrain to suit all skill levels, cycling is a fantastic way to explore the area at your own pace.

Rock climbing in Paklenica national park

For adrenaline junkies seeking an exhilarating challenge, head to nearby Paklenica National Park for world-class rock-climbing opportunities. Climb rugged limestone cliffs, test your skills on diverse routes, and enjoy breath-taking views of the Adriatic Sea and surrounding mountains.

Sailing excursions

Experience the Adriatic Sea in style with a sailing excursion departing from Skradin. Join a guided tour or charter your own yacht and set sail to explore hidden coves, remote islands, and secluded beaches. Enjoy snorkelling in crystal-clear waters, sunbathing on deck, and indulging in delicious local cuisine prepared by your onboard chef.

Birdwatching in Vrana lake nature park

Just a short drive from Skradin lies Vrana Lake Nature Park, a haven for birdwatchers. Explore the diverse habitats around the largest lake in Croatia, home to over 250 species of birds. Keep your binoculars handy as you spot herons, egrets, ospreys, and even the rare Eurasian bittern in their natural habitat.

Horseback riding in the Dalmatian hinterland

Saddle up and embark on a horseback riding adventure through the scenic landscapes of the Dalmatian Hinterland. Follow winding trails that lead through olive groves, vineyards, and rolling hills, enjoying the peaceful rhythm of your horse's hoofbeats. It is a unique way to connect with nature and experience the beauty of the Croatian countryside.

Scuba diving in the Adriatic Sea

Dive into the crystal-clear waters of the Adriatic Sea and discover a vibrant underwater world teeming with marine life. Join a guided scuba diving excursion to explore colourful reefs, underwater caves, and fascinating shipwrecks. With visibility often exceeding 30 meters, the Adriatic offers excellent diving conditions for divers of all levels.

Zip-lining in Omis

For an adrenaline-fueled adventure, venture to Omis and experience the thrill of zip-lining high above the Cetina River canyon. Soar through the air at speeds of up to 65 kilometres per hour, taking in panoramic views of the surrounding mountains and forests below.

Cycling along the Krka River

Rent a bike and pedal your way along the scenic trails that follow the meandering path of the Krka River. As you cycle through lush forests and charming villages, you'll encounter picturesque waterfalls and panoramic viewpoints. It is a leisurely way to explore the natural beauty of the region while enjoying the fresh air and tranquillity of the countryside.

Rock climbing in Paklenica national park

Just a short drive from Skradin, Paklenica National Park offers world-class rock-climbing opportunities amidst stunning limestone cliffs. Whether you are a seasoned climber or a novice looking to try something new, the park's diverse range of routes caters to climbers of all skill levels.

Sea kayaking along the Dalmatian coast

Embark on a sea kayaking adventure along the rugged coastline of the Dalmatian Coast, exploring hidden coves, sea caves, and secluded beaches. Paddle beneath towering cliffs and crystal-clear waters, keeping an eye out for marine life such as dolphins and sea turtles.

Hiking in Krka national park

Lace up your hiking boots and set out to explore the scenic trails of Krka National Park, home to stunning waterfalls, lush forests, and diverse wildlife. Choose from a variety of hiking routes that wind through the park's pristine landscapes, offering opportunities to immerse yourself in nature and discover hidden gems along the way.

After a day of outdoor exploration, return to Skradin and unwind in the charming town centre, where quaint cafes and restaurants beckon with delicious local cuisine and refreshing drinks. Reflect on the day's adventures as you watch the sun set over the Krka River, casting a golden glow across the tranquil waters. With its endless opportunities for outdoor recreation and natural beauty, Skradin is a hidden gem waiting to be discovered by adventurous travellers.

Echoes of riverside joy: Embracing traditions in Skradin

Welcome to Skradin, a picturesque town nestled along the banks of the Krka River in the heart of Croatia. As you explore the cobblestone streets and historic landmarks, you'll discover a vibrant cultural scene and a deep sense of tradition woven into the fabric of everyday life. From colourful festivals celebrating the town's maritime heritage to gastronomic events showcasing the region's culinary delights, Skradin offers a rich tapestry of local traditions and experiences waiting to be explored.

Skradinski Vezovi (July/August)

Celebrated annually in July, Skradinski Vezovi is a traditional festival that pays homage to the town's rich maritime history and cultural heritage. Visitors can enjoy a colourful procession of decorated boats sailing along the Krka River, accompanied by live music, dance performances, and local cuisine. The festival also features exhibitions showcasing traditional crafts and skills, offering insight into Skradin's maritime traditions.

Dani Mira (August)

Dani Mira is an annual event held in September that celebrates peace, tolerance, and multiculturalism. The festival features cultural performances, art exhibitions, and workshops promoting dialogue and understanding among different communities. Visitors can participate in discussions on global issues, attend film screenings, and enjoy concerts showcasing diverse musical genres.

Noć Glazbe (July/August)

Noć Glazbe is a music festival held during the summer months, featuring a variety of live performances ranging from traditional Croatian music to contemporary genres. The streets of Skradin come alive with the sounds of music as local bands and artists entertain audiences late into the night.

Mala Gospa (September)

Mala Gospa, or the Feast of the Nativity of the Virgin Mary, is a religious celebration observed in Skradin with solemn processions, church services, and cultural performances. The town's streets are adorned with colourful decorations, and locals gather to pay homage to the patron saint of Skradin.

Fešta od Piva (July/August)

Held in August, Fešta od Piva is a lively beer festival that brings together locals and visitors alike to enjoy a wide selection of craft beers from across Croatia and beyond. The festival atmosphere is enhanced by live music, street performances, and delicious food stalls offering traditional Croatian dishes.

Dan Grada (June/July/August)

Dan Grada, or Town Day, is an annual celebration that honours the founding of Skradin and its importance in Croatian history. The festivities include concerts, art exhibitions, and traditional craft demonstrations, showcasing the town's cultural heritage. Locals take pride in their town's legacy, and visitors are warmly welcomed to join in the festivities and experience the vibrant spirit of Skradin.

Ribarska Fešta (August)

Ribarska Fešta, or the Fishermen's Festival, is a celebration of Skradin's maritime heritage and the bounty of the Adriatic Sea. Held annually, this festival features traditional seafood dishes prepared by local fishermen, live music, and folk dances. Visitors can savour freshly caught fish and seafood delicacies while enjoying the festive ambiance along the waterfront.

Noć Muzeja (May/June)

Noć Muzeja, or Museum Night, is an annual cultural event that takes place in Skradin's museums and galleries. On this special night, these cultural institutions open their doors to the public free of charge, offering guided tours, art exhibitions, and interactive workshops. Visitors can explore Skradin's rich history and artistic heritage while engaging with local artists and historians.

Ljeto na Obali (June-August)

Ljeto na Obali, or Summer on the Coast, is a series of summer events and festivals that enliven Skradin's waterfront during the warmer months. From open-air concerts and film screenings to food and wine festivals, there is something for everyone to enjoy. Locals and visitors alike gather by the sea to soak up the sun, savour delicious cuisine, and revel in the vibrant atmosphere of summer in Skradin.

Krštenje Brodova (April/May)

Krštenje Brodova, or Boat Baptism, is a unique maritime tradition celebrated in Skradin, where newly built boats are christened and blessed for safe voyages. The ceremony is accompanied by music, dancing, and feasting, as the local community gathers to witness this symbolic ritual. Visitors can partake in the festivities and gain insight into the seafaring culture of Skradin.

As you bid farewell to Skradin, take with you the memories of its lively festivals and cherished traditions, each one adding a layer of depth to your experience in this charming town. Whether you danced the night away at Noć Glazbe or savoured the flavours of truffle-infused dishes during Truffle Days, Skradin has left an indelible mark on your heart. As you journey onward, may the spirit of Skradin's traditions continue to inspire and enrich your travels wherever they may take you.

Secrets of successful exploration: Tips for exploring Skradin

Welcome to Skradin, a picturesque town nestled along the banks of the Krka River in Croatia. As you embark on your journey to this charming destination, allow us to provide you with some invaluable travel tips to ensure a memorable and seamless experience. From exploring historic landmarks to indulging in culinary delights and engaging in outdoor adventures, Skradin offers a diverse range of attractions waiting to be discovered. Let these travel tips serve as your guide to unlocking the beauty and culture of Skradin, making your visit truly unforgettable.

Indulge in Wine Tasting

Skradin lies in the heart of the Dalmatian wine region, making it the perfect destination for wine enthusiasts. Embark on a wine tasting tour to discover the region's rich viticultural heritage and sample a variety of local wines. Visit family-owned wineries nestled among the rolling hills and vineyards, where you'll have the opportunity to taste indigenous grape varietals such as Babic and Plavac Mali.

Stroll Through the Old Town

Take a leisurely stroll through the cobblestone streets of Skradin's Old Town and soak up the town's historic charm. Admire the well-preserved architecture of centuries-old buildings adorned with colourful shutters and flower-filled balconies. Discover hidden gems around every corner, from quaint cafes and artisan shops to ancient churches and medieval fortifications.

Venture to Visovac Island

Escape the hustle and bustle of mainland Skradin with a tranquil boat trip to Visovac Island, located in the heart of the Krka River. As you glide across the serene waters, you'll be greeted by the sight of the island's picturesque Franciscan monastery nestled amidst lush greenery. Step ashore and explore the island's peaceful grounds, where fragrant gardens and ancient olive groves provide a serene setting for reflection and relaxation.

Take a Boat Tour of Krka River

Explore the pristine waters of the Krka River with a scenic boat tour departing from Skradin. Cruise along the river's meandering channels and marvel at the lush vegetation and diverse wildlife that line its banks. As you glide past hidden coves and secluded beaches, soak in the tranquillity of this idyllic setting and capture unforgettable moments against the backdrop of dramatic cliffs and verdant forests.

Hike to Skradinski Buk Waterfall

Lace up your hiking boots and embark on a thrilling trek to Skradinski Buk, one of the most breath-taking waterfalls in Krka National Park. Follow the well-marked trails that wind through dense woodlands and across wooden footbridges, offering panoramic views of the cascading falls and surrounding landscape.

Visit Burnum Archaeological Site

Delve into Skradin's rich history with a visit to the nearby Burnum Archaeological Site, where ancient Roman ruins offer a glimpse into the region's past. Explore the remains of a Roman military camp, amphitheater, and aqueduct, marvelling at the architectural feats of the ancient civilization that once thrived here. Learn about the site's significance as a strategic military outpost and cultural centre, and imagine life in Roman times as you wander among the ancient ruins.

Attend the Feast of St. Roko

Experience the vibrant traditions of Skradin by attending the Feast of St. Roko, a popular religious festival held annually in August. Join locals and visitors alike in celebrating the patron saint of the town with a festive procession, traditional music, and dance performances. Sample delicious local delicacies and sweet treats at the bustling food stalls that line the streets, and immerse yourself in the lively atmosphere of this cultural celebration.

Cycle the Krka River Bike Trail

Strap on your helmet and embark on a cycling adventure along the scenic Krka River Bike Trail, which winds its way through the picturesque landscapes of Krka National Park. Pedal past lush forests, meandering rivers, and hidden waterfalls as you explore the park's diverse ecosystems and abundant wildlife.

Relax on the Beaches of Sibenik Riviera

Escape the hustle and bustle of city life and unwind on the pristine beaches of the nearby Sibenik Riviera. From secluded coves and hidden bays to lively resort towns, the coastline offers a variety of options for sunbathing, swimming, and water sports.

As the sun sets on your time in Skradin, take with you cherished memories of its natural beauty, rich history, and warm hospitality. Whether you spent your days exploring waterfalls, savouring local cuisine, or immersing yourself in cultural festivities, Skradin will forever hold a special place in your heart. Until we meet again, may your travels be filled with adventure and discovery.

Saying goodbye to serenity: Skradin's legacy lives on in memories

With Skradin fading into the horizon, you find yourself enveloped in a warm embrace of memories, a collection of moments that have left an indelible mark on your heart. The town's ancient charm, woven into the fabric of its historic streets, has whispered tales of the past, inviting you to explore the rich tapestry of its cultural heritage. The breath-taking beauty of the Krka National Park has awakened your senses, immersing you in a symphony of nature's wonders that resonate within. The warmth of the locals, the flavours of traditional cuisine, and the serenity of the coastal and river vistas have intertwined to create a mosaic of experiences that linger in your memory, evoking a sense of gratitude and inspiration for the beauty and magic found in this hidden gem.

In Skradin, you have discovered a place where history, nature, and human connection converge in a harmonious dance, inviting you to immerse yourself in the rhythm of its enchanting streets, the vibrant colours of its landscapes, and the genuine warmth of its community. The town's ability to captivate your senses, stir your emotions, and ignite your imagination has left a lasting impression, inviting you to carry the essence of Skradin with you as you venture forth. Whether you are reminiscing about the historic Old Town, the majestic Krka waterfalls, or the tranquil beauty of the coastal landscapes, Skradin's closing thoughts are a symphony of experiences that echo within, enchanting your soul and inspiring future journeys.

Jay Chandarana

Korcula: Vineyards and seascapes

Unveiling Korcula: Island serenity amidst coastal grandeur

Korčula, a vibrant island gem nestled in the crystal-clear waters of the Adriatic Sea, is a place where history, culture, and natural beauty converge in a captivating dance. With roots steeped in ancient civilizations, the island's rich cultural heritage is reflected in its well-preserved architecture, narrow cobblestone streets, and the remnants of its medieval walls. The town of Korčula, the island's namesake and a jewel in its own right, exudes a unique charm that captivates visitors with its enchanting blend of history, art, and coastal landscapes.

Korčula's allure extends beyond its historic streets, as the island's lush forests, pristine beaches, and crystal-clear waters offer a stunning backdrop for outdoor adventures and relaxation. The town's vibrant arts scene, coupled with its delectable culinary offerings, adds a contemporary flair to this coastal gem, inviting travellers to indulge in a sensory journey that encompasses the best of both history and nature. Whether exploring the historic Old Town, indulging in local delicacies at charming cafes, or embarking on a boat tour to witness the island's breath-taking beauty, Korčula promises a journey filled with cultural immersion, scenic wonders, and moments of serenity along the Dalmatian coast.

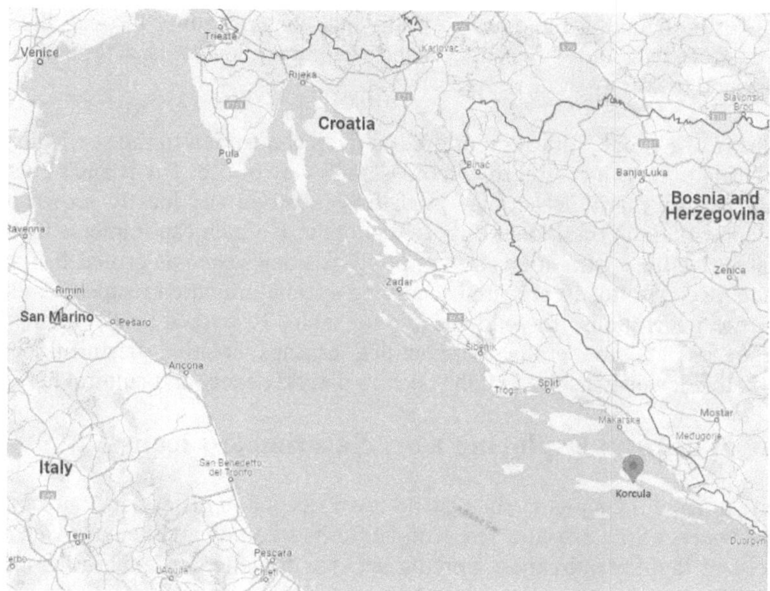

Echoes of island majesty: Korcula's maritime legacy

Situated on the Adriatic Sea, Korcula Island boasts a rich tapestry of historical significance that spans millennia. Believed to have been inhabited since prehistoric times, Korcula's strategic location along ancient trade routes made it a coveted prize for many civilizations throughout history. One of the island's most notable claims to fame is its association with the legendary explorer Marco Polo, who is said to have been born within the walls of Korcula's Old Town. The town's medieval fortifications and Renaissance architecture bear witness to its illustrious past as a Venetian stronghold, serving as a testament to its enduring significance in the region.

Korcula's historical significance is further underscored by its role as a cultural crossroads, where East meets West in a vibrant tapestry of influences. Over the centuries, the island has been shaped by the successive waves of Greek, Roman, Byzantine, Venetian, and Ottoman rule, each leaving their mark on its cultural landscape. From the imposing walls of Korcula's Old Town to the intricate stone carvings adorning its churches and palaces, the island's architecture tells the story of its tumultuous history and the resilience of its people. Today, Korcula stands as a living monument to its past, offering visitors a glimpse into the rich tapestry of cultures that have shaped its identity over the centuries.

Island rhythms: Embracing Korcula's cultural beat

Korcula's local culture is a vibrant mosaic of traditions, folklore, and customs that have been passed down through generations. Rooted in its ancient heritage and shaped by centuries of maritime trade, the island's culture is a reflection of its unique position at the crossroads of the Adriatic. From the lively folk dances performed during summer festivals to the haunting melodies of traditional songs echoing through the narrow streets of Korcula's Old Town, the island's cultural identity is a testament to the resilience and creativity of its people.

At the heart of Korcula's local culture lies a deep connection to the sea, with fishing and seafaring playing a central role in the island's way of life. The island's cuisine is a celebration of its maritime heritage, with fresh seafood and locally grown produce taking centre stage in traditional dishes. Visitors to Korcula can immerse themselves in the island's culinary traditions by sampling delicacies such as grilled fish, octopus salad, and black risotto, all prepared according to time-honoured recipes passed down through the generations. Beyond the dining table, Korcula's local culture is also evident in its arts and crafts, with skilled artisans creating beautiful ceramics, lacework, and jewelry inspired by the island's natural beauty and cultural heritage.

Legacy of beauty: Exploring Korcula's timeless icons

Welcome to Korčula, a picturesque island town steeped in history and surrounded by the azure waters of the Adriatic Sea. Known for its stunning architecture, rich cultural heritage, and idyllic landscapes, Korčula beckons travellers to explore its charming streets and discover its many landmarks and points of interest. From medieval fortresses and ancient cathedrals to tranquil beaches and scenic viewpoints, there is no shortage of attractions to captivate your imagination and immerse you in the beauty of this enchanting destination.

Marco Polo house

Explore the birthplace of one of history's most famous explorers at the Marco Polo House, a traditional stone building believed to be the childhood home of Marco Polo. Learn about the life and adventures of this legendary figure through interactive exhibits, artifacts, and multimedia presentations.

Korcula town walls

Ascend the ancient ramparts that encircle Korčula's Old Town and marvel at the breath-taking views of the Adriatic Sea and nearby archipelago. Dating back to the 13th century, the town walls offer a glimpse into Korčula's rich maritime history and strategic importance as a fortified settlement.

Korcula old town

Step back in time as you wander through the narrow cobblestone streets of Korčula's Old Town, a beautifully preserved medieval settlement dating back to the 13th century. Marvel at the elegant Venetian architecture, fortified walls, and historic buildings adorned with intricate stonework. Do not miss the chance to visit the iconic St. Mark's Cathedral, an impressive Gothic-Renaissance masterpiece featuring stunning artworks and a bell tower offering panoramic views of the town and surrounding islands.

Korcula town museum

Delve into the rich history and culture of Korčula at the town museum, housed within the majestic Gabrielis Palace. Explore fascinating exhibits showcasing archaeological finds, historical artifacts, and works of art that chronicle the island's past from ancient times to the present day. Admire intricate woodcarvings, traditional costumes, and maritime memorabilia, and gain insights into Korčula's enduring legacy as a centre of trade, craftsmanship, and artistic expression.

Tower Revelin

Ascend the stone steps of Tower Revelin, a centuries-old defensive tower perched on the eastern edge of Korčula's Old Town. Marvel at the commanding views of the surrounding sea and coastline from this strategic vantage point, which once served as a lookout and signalling station to protect the town from maritime threats.

Przina beach

Escape to the pristine shores of Pržina Beach, located on the southern coast of Korčula near the village of Lumbarda. Sink your toes into the soft golden sands and soak up the Mediterranean sunshine as you relax by the tranquil waters of the Adriatic Sea. Take a refreshing dip in the crystal-clear sea or try your hand at water sports such as kayaking, paddleboarding, or windsurfing against the backdrop of scenic vineyards and olive groves.

St. Mark's cathedral

Marvel at the exquisite architecture and artistic treasures of St. Mark's Cathedral, the spiritual and cultural centrepiece of Korčula's Old Town. Built in the Venetian Gothic style during the 15th and 16th centuries, this majestic cathedral is dedicated to St. Mark, the patron saint of Venice, and features a stunning facade adorned with intricate stone carvings and sculptures. Step inside to admire the cathedral's richly decorated interior, which includes works by renowned Renaissance artists such as Tintoretto and Paolo Veneziano, as well as a beautifully carved wooden choir screen.

Lumbarda vineyards

Venture to the picturesque village of Lumbarda, located just a short drive from Korčula, and explore its renowned vineyards and wineries. Known for producing Grk, a unique white wine varietal indigenous to the island, Lumbarda invites visitors to sample its award-winning wines and learn about the traditional winemaking methods passed down through generations.

Korcula town hall

Discover the architectural elegance and historical significance of Korčula Town Hall, an imposing Renaissance building located in the heart of the Old Town square. Originally constructed in the 15th century as a Venetian palace, the Town Hall served as the seat of municipal government and a centre of civic life for centuries. Admire the building's ornate facade, adorned with decorative elements such as coats of arms, stone carvings, and elegant balconies, and explore its interior chambers, including the council chamber, mayor's office, and assembly hall, which are still used for official ceremonies and events today.

Church of St. Peter

Discover the Church of St. Peter, a charming Romanesque church located just outside the Old Town walls. Dating back to the 11th century, this historic church features a simple yet elegant facade adorned with carved stone reliefs and a distinctive bell tower. Step inside to admire the church's beautifully preserved interior, which includes ancient frescoes, intricate altarpieces, and a serene atmosphere conducive to reflection and contemplation.

Badija island monastery

Take a short boat ride from Korčula to Badija Island and explore the ruins of a Franciscan monastery dating back to the 15th century. Located amidst lush pine forests and pristine beaches, this tranquil island sanctuary offers a peaceful retreat from the hustle and bustle of Korčula Town. Wander through the monastery's cloisters, chapels, and gardens, and soak up the serene beauty of this secluded island paradise.

As your journey through Korčula comes to an end, reflect on the timeless beauty and captivating allure of this historic island town. Whether you've explored its medieval streets, marvelled at its architectural wonders, or savoured its culinary delights, Korčula has left an indelible mark on your heart and soul. As you bid farewell to this enchanting destination, carry with you the memories of its storied past and the promise of future adventures yet to unfold amidst the sun-drenched landscapes of the Adriatic coast.

Savouring Korcula: Culinary chronicles of the island

Embark on a culinary journey through Korčula, where traditional flavours blend with Mediterranean influences to create a gastronomic paradise. From fresh seafood caught in the pristine waters of the Adriatic to locally sourced ingredients bursting with flavour, Korčula's culinary scene offers a feast for the senses. Indulge in the island's culinary delights as you savour each mouth-watering dish and uncover the secrets of its rich culinary heritage.

Pasticada

Sink your teeth into pašticada, a hearty beef stew slow-cooked in a flavourful marinade of red wine, vinegar, and herbs. This traditional Dalmatian dish is typically served with homemade gnocchi or creamy mashed potatoes, allowing the tender meat to melt in your mouth with each savoury bite.

Ston oysters

Treat your taste buds to the briny goodness of Ston oysters, renowned for their plump texture and exquisite flavour. Harvested from the pristine waters of nearby Ston Bay, these delectable bivalves are best enjoyed freshly shucked with a squeeze of lemon or a drizzle of local olive oil.

Korcula lamb

Savour the succulent flavours of Korčula lamb, raised on the island's lush pastures and seasoned with aromatic herbs and spices. Grilled to perfection over an open flame or slow-roasted until tender, Korčula lamb is a culinary delight that showcases the island's agricultural bounty. Accompanied by seasonal vegetables and a glass of local wine, this hearty dish is sure to satisfy even the most discerning palates.

Grilled octopus

Delight in the tender texture and smoky flavour of grilled octopus, a beloved delicacy in Korčula's coastal cuisine. Marinated in olive oil, garlic, and herbs, the octopus is cooked over an open flame until charred and caramelized, creating a mouth-watering dish that pairs perfectly with a squeeze of lemon and a glass of local wine.

Black risotto

Sample Korčula's signature dish, black risotto, made with tender cuttlefish, savoury squid ink, and aromatic spices. This unique delicacy boasts a rich, velvety texture and a distinct umami flavour, thanks to the infusion of squid ink. Served piping hot and garnished with fresh parsley, black risotto is a must-try for seafood enthusiasts seeking an authentic taste of the Adriatic.

Zrnovski Makaruni

Taste the traditional pasta of Korčula, known as Žrnovski makaruni, handmade with care by local artisans. These thick, hand-rolled noodles are crafted from a simple dough of flour and water, then cooked until al dente and served with a variety of sauces, from rich meat ragu to tangy tomato and basil.

Korcula smoked ham

Delight in the rich and smoky flavours of Korčula's prized smoked ham, known locally as pršut. Crafted from high-quality Dalmatian pork and seasoned with sea salt, pršut is cured and air-dried in the island's Mediterranean climate, resulting in a tender and savoury delicacy. Sliced thinly and served alongside crusty bread, cheese, and olives, Korčula pršut is a quintessential component of any Croatian charcuterie board, offering a taste of tradition with every bite.

Soparnik

Experience a taste of Croatia's culinary heritage with soparnik, a traditional savoury pie that originated in the Dalmatian region. Made from layers of thin dough filled with a mixture of Swiss chard, onions, and garlic, soparnik is baked until golden and crispy, resulting in a satisfying and flavourful dish. Enjoyed as both a snack and a main course, soparnik reflects the simplicity and authenticity of Dalmatian cuisine, making it a must-try for food enthusiasts visiting Korčula.

Korcula white wine

Indulge in the crisp and refreshing white wines produced on the island of Korčula, celebrated for their bright acidity and fruity aromas. Made from indigenous grape varieties such as pošip and grk, Korčula white wines are the perfect accompaniment to the region's seafood-centric cuisine. Sip a glass of chilled pošip as you admire the sunset over the Adriatic Sea, and discover why Korčula's wine heritage is a source of pride for locals and a delight for visitors.

Korcula seafood risotto

Indulge in the flavours of the Adriatic with Korčula's seafood risotto, a classic dish that showcases the region's bounty of fresh seafood and aromatic herbs. Made with locally sourced ingredients such as mussels, shrimp, and squid, Korčula seafood risotto is cooked to creamy perfection with Arborio rice, white wine, and fish stock. Garnished with parsley and a squeeze of lemon, this savoury dish is a true taste of the sea and a favourite among visitors to the island.

As you explore Korčula's culinary delights, you'll discover a tapestry of flavours that reflect the island's rich culinary heritage and natural abundance. From savoury seafood dishes to sweet treats made with love, each bite offers a taste of tradition and a glimpse into the vibrant culture of Korčula. Whether dining in a cozy tavern or sampling street food by the sea, let the flavours of Korčula linger on your palate and inspire your culinary adventures for years to come.

Gems of solitude: Unveiling Korcula's secluded charms

Nestled amidst the azure waters of the Adriatic Sea, Korčula is a treasure trove of hidden gems waiting to be discovered. From secluded beaches and secret coves to hidden alleys and ancient ruins, this enchanting island offers a wealth of hidden delights for intrepid travellers to explore. Join us as we unveil some of Korčula's best-kept secrets, revealing the hidden gems that lie off the beaten path.

Sveti Antun beach

This secluded beach is a paradise for those seeking tranquillity and natural beauty. With its pristine waters and soft sands, Sveti Antun Beach offers a serene escape from the bustling tourist areas. Surrounded by lush greenery and accessible only by boat or a scenic hike, it provides an intimate setting for sunbathing, swimming, and snorkelling.

Račišće village

Tucked away on the northern coast of Korčula, Račišće Village is a charming seaside hamlet that epitomizes traditional Dalmatian life. Its idyllic setting, with colourful fishing boats bobbing in the harbour and stone houses lining the waterfront, exudes a sense of timeless beauty.

Pupnat village

Nestled in the heart of Korčula, Pupnat Village is a hidden gem that exudes charm and authenticity. Its stone houses and narrow streets evoke a sense of old-world charm, while its rustic taverns serve up traditional Dalmatian cuisine made from locally sourced ingredients.

Žrnovo village

Just a short drive inland from Korčula Town lies the quaint village of Žrnovo, renowned for its picturesque scenery and rich cultural heritage. Surrounded by vineyards and olive groves, Žrnovo offers a glimpse into traditional island life, with its stone houses and ancient churches dotting the landscape.

Bilin Žal beach

Tucked away on the southern coast of Korčula, Bilin Žal Beach is a hidden gem beloved by locals and intrepid travellers alike. Accessible via a scenic coastal path or a short boat ride from Korčula Town, this secluded cove boasts crystal-clear waters and pebble shores, perfect for swimming, snorkelling, and sunbathing in peace.

Sveti Nikola church

Perched atop a hill overlooking the town of Blato, Sveti Nikola Church is a hidden architectural gem with a rich history. Dating back to the 15th century, the church features a striking bell tower and well-preserved frescoes that provide insights into Korčula's religious and cultural heritage.

Zakerjan tower

Nestled within the labyrinthine streets of Korčula Old Town, Zakerjan Tower stands as a testament to the island's medieval past. Built in the 15th century as a defensive stronghold, this cylindrical tower offers a fascinating glimpse into Korčula's architectural heritage. Visitors can ascend its narrow staircase to reach the top, where panoramic views of the town and surrounding sea await.

Raznjic lighthouse

Located on the western tip of Korčula Island, Raznjic Lighthouse is a hidden gem that beckons adventurers to its remote shores. Accessible only by boat or a rugged hiking trail, this 19th-century lighthouse offers a secluded escape from the hustle and bustle of modern life. Surrounded by pristine nature and rugged cliffs,

Proizd Island

A short boat ride from Korčula's mainland, Proizd Island is a hidden paradise known for its pristine beaches and crystal-clear waters. Accessible only by private boat or water taxi, Proizd offers a secluded escape from the crowds, with several secluded coves and rocky outcrops to explore. Visitors can swim, snorkel, or simply bask in the sun on Proizd's sun-drenched shores, immersing themselves in the natural beauty of this unspoiled island.

Vela Spila cave

Situated near the village of Vela Luka on the western side of Korčula Island, Vela Spila Cave is an archaeological marvel shrouded in mystery and intrigue. Dating back to the Paleolithic era, this expansive cave complex contains traces of ancient human habitation, including tools, pottery, and artwork. Guided tours of Vela Spila offer visitors a fascinating journey through time, allowing them to explore the cave's chambers and learn about its significance in prehistoric culture.

As you bid farewell to Korčula, take with you the memories of its hidden gems – the secret beaches, hidden alleys, and ancient ruins that speak to the island's rich history and natural beauty. Whether you've explored its secluded coves, climbed its medieval towers, or wandered through its quaint villages, Korčula will forever hold a special place in your heart as a true hidden gem of the Adriatic.

Trailblazing Korcula: Outdoor thrills along the coast

Nestled in the heart of the Adriatic Sea, the island of Korčula offers a playground of outdoor adventures for nature lovers and thrill-seekers alike. From hiking along scenic trails to exploring hidden coves and indulging in water sports, Korčula's diverse landscape provides endless opportunities for outdoor exploration and excitement. Whether you prefer to soar above the waves or immerse yourself in the island's lush forests, there is something for everyone to enjoy amidst Korčula's stunning natural beauty.

Hiking and biking

Korčula boasts a network of scenic hiking and biking trails that wind through olive groves, vineyards, and rugged coastal landscapes. Explore the island's diverse terrain on foot or by bike, with trails ranging from leisurely coastal paths to challenging mountain routes.

Kayaking and paddleboarding

Embark on a kayaking or paddleboarding adventure along Korčula's pristine coastline, where crystal-clear waters and secluded bays await. Paddle past hidden coves, sea caves, and rocky islets, discovering secluded beaches and wildlife along the way.

Snorkelling and scuba diving

Dive into the turquoise waters of the Adriatic Sea and discover Korčula's vibrant underwater world teeming with marine life and colourful reefs. Explore dive sites such as the Badija Reef and the Vela Cave, where you'll encounter schools of fish, octopuses, and even the occasional dolphin.

Windsurfing and kitesurfing

Feel the wind in your sails as you windsurf or kitesurf across the azure waters surrounding Korčula. With consistent winds and favourable conditions, the island's coastal areas provide an ideal playground for wind-driven water sports. Test your skills at spots like Viganj and Pelješac, where you can ride the waves and catch air while taking in stunning views of the Dalmatian coastline.

Sailing and boat tours

Set sail on a boat tour around the islands of the Korčula archipelago, where you'll discover hidden bays, secluded beaches, and charming fishing villages. Join a guided sailing excursion or rent a private boat to explore at your own pace, stopping to swim, snorkel, and enjoy delicious seafood along the way.

Rock climbing

Challenge yourself on Korčula's rugged cliffs and limestone formations, perfect for rock climbing enthusiasts of all levels. The island offers a variety of climbing routes with stunning views of the Adriatic Sea, providing an exhilarating experience for adventurers seeking vertical thrills.

Cycling tours

Join a cycling tour and explore the scenic beauty of Korčula at a leisurely pace. Pedal through picturesque villages, vineyards, and olive groves, stopping to sample local delicacies and wine along the way. With guided tours available for all skill levels, cycling is an excellent way to discover the island's hidden gems and charming countryside.

Birdwatching

Discover Korčula's rich birdlife as you embark on a birdwatching excursion through its diverse habitats. From wetlands and forests to coastal cliffs, the island is home to a wide variety of bird species, including herons, eagles, and migratory birds. Grab your binoculars and explore the island's natural wonders while spotting colourful feathered inhabitants.

Yoga and wellness retreats

Rejuvenate your mind, body, and soul with a yoga and wellness retreat amidst Korčula's serene surroundings. Join daily yoga sessions led by experienced instructors, practice meditation, and indulge in spa treatments inspired by the island's natural ingredients.

Sea kayaking

Explore the crystal-clear waters surrounding Korčula on a sea kayaking adventure. Paddle along the island's rugged coastline, weaving through hidden coves, secluded beaches, and ancient sea caves. With experienced guides leading the way, you'll have the opportunity to discover remote corners of the island while enjoying the serenity of the Adriatic Sea.

Stand-up paddleboarding

Experience the beauty of Korčula's coastline from a unique perspective as you glide across the water on a stand-up paddleboard. Whether you are cruising along the calm waters of the bay or exploring hidden coves and sea caves, SUP offers a fun and adventurous way to explore the island's scenic shores.

From land to sea, Korčula offers a myriad of outdoor activities that allow visitors to immerse themselves in the island's natural splendour. Whether you are hiking along scenic trails, paddling through crystal-clear waters, or sailing around hidden coves, each adventure promises unforgettable experiences and breath-taking views. Explore the great outdoors of Korčula and discover the endless wonders that await amidst its stunning landscapes and pristine waters.

Traditions awaken: Korcula's rich cultural tapestry

Immerse yourself in the rich cultural heritage of Korčula by experiencing its vibrant local traditions and festivals. From centuries-old customs to lively celebrations, these events offer a glimpse into the island's unique identity and spirit. Join locals and visitors alike as they come together to honour tradition, celebrate community, and revel in the magic of Korčula's cultural tapestry.

Festival Marko Polo (September)

The Marco Polo Festival pays homage to one of Korčula's most famous sons, the legendary explorer Marco Polo. Held annually, this festival celebrates the island's maritime legacy and Marco Polo's adventurous spirit through a series of lively events and performances. Visitors can enjoy historical re-enactments, traditional music and dance, as well as culinary delights inspired by Marco Polo's travels.

Kumpanija (June/July)

The Kumpanija is a traditional sword dance that originated in the Dalmatian region and is still practiced in Korčula today. This ancient martial dance is performed by a group of dancers known as 'kumpani' who showcase their skill and agility with swords. Accompanied by traditional music, the Kumpanija is a dynamic, captivating spectacle that reflects the island's proud martial heritage and is often performed during religious festivals and special occasions.

Ljetni Kalendar Mjuzikla (June-August)

The Korčula Summer Festival, known locally as Ljetni Kalendar Mjuzikla, is a highlight of the island's cultural calendar. Held annually from June to September, this festival features a diverse program of music, theatre, dance, and art, showcasing both local talent and international performers. Visitors can enjoy open-air concerts, theatre productions, art exhibitions, and street performances throughout the historic streets of Korčula.

Likovna Kolonija (June-August)

The Korčula Art Colony, or Likovna Kolonija, is an annual gathering of artists from Croatia and beyond who come together to create and exhibit their work in the picturesque surroundings of Korčula. Established in the 1950s, the art colony has become a renowned cultural event, attracting painters, sculptors, photographers, and other artists who are inspired by the island's natural beauty and rich cultural heritage. During the colony, artists have the opportunity to collaborate, exchange ideas, and showcase their creations in exhibitions and public installations.

Korčulanski Moreska (June-September)

The Korčula Sword Dance, known locally as Korčulanski Moreska, is a traditional dance that has been performed on the island for centuries. It is a symbolic re-enactment of a battle between two kings, the Red King and the Black King, over a beautiful maiden. Dancers, clad in elaborate costumes and wielding swords, perform intricate choreography to the beat of traditional music.

Ribarske Noći (June to August)

Korčula Fishermen's Nights, or Ribarske Noći, are evening events held during the summer months, celebrating the island's maritime heritage and the bounty of the Adriatic Sea. Organized in different villages and towns along the coast, these traditional gatherings bring together locals and visitors to enjoy freshly caught seafood, grilled to perfection and served with local wines and traditional accompaniments. Visitors can dine al fresco by the waterfront, surrounded by the sights and sounds of the sea, while local musicians provide entertainment with traditional songs and melodies.

Dan Grada Korčule (June/July)

Korčula Day, or Dan Grada Korčule, is an annual celebration commemorating the founding of the town of Korčula. Held on September 6th, the feast day of St. Mark, the patron saint of Korčula, this festive occasion brings together locals and visitors to honour the town's history and heritage. The day begins with a religious procession and a mass at the St. Mark's Cathedral, followed by traditional performances, cultural activities, and culinary delights throughout the town. Visitors can explore historical landmarks, artisanal markets, and exhibitions showcasing Korčula's rich cultural legacy.

Etno Noć (June to August)

Korčula Ethno Night is an enchanting event that celebrates the island's rich cultural heritage and traditional folk music and dance. Held in the summer months, usually in July or August, this lively gathering brings together local folk musicians, singers, and dancers who showcase the vibrant rhythms and melodies of Korčula's musical traditions. Visitors can experience authentic performances of klapa singing, tamburitza music, and traditional dances such as the mafrina and the moštra. The event often includes workshops, demonstrations, and opportunities for audience participation, allowing visitors to immerse themselves in the spirit of Korčula's folk culture and create lasting memories of their island experience.

Korčulanski Barokni Festival (September)

The Korčula Music Festival, also known as the Korčula Baroque Festival, is an annual event dedicated to classical music, particularly the Baroque repertoire. Held in various historic venues across the town, including churches, palaces, and open-air squares, the festival features performances by renowned international and local musicians, orchestras, and chamber ensembles. Audiences can enjoy concerts, recitals, and opera productions showcasing masterpieces by composers such as Vivaldi, Bach, and Handel, performed with authenticity and passion.

From the ancient sword dance of Moreska to the spirited celebrations of the Korčula Carnival, the island's local traditions and festivals offer a window into its rich cultural heritage and vibrant community spirit. Whether you are captivated by the dramatic re-enactments of historical battles or swept up in the joyous atmosphere of carnival festivities, each event promises a memorable and immersive experience that will leave you enchanted by the magic of Korčula.

Insider insights: Navigating Korcula's charms like a local

Welcome to Korčula, a captivating island in the Adriatic Sea known for its rich history, stunning natural beauty, and vibrant cultural scene. Whether you are exploring the cobblestone streets of Old Town Korčula, sampling local wines at family-owned wineries, or soaking up the sun on secluded beaches, this enchanting destination offers endless opportunities for adventure and relaxation. To help you make the most of your visit, here are some essential travel tips for experiencing the best of Korčula.

Visit local wineries

Embark on a wine-tasting journey through Korčula's renowned vineyards, where the island's unique terroir produces exceptional wines. Sample indigenous grape varieties such as Pošip, Grk, and Plavac Mali, renowned for their distinct flavours and aromas. Meet passionate winemakers who will guide you through the tasting process, sharing insights into their traditional winemaking techniques and the island's viticultural heritage.

Take a boat trip

Set sail on the crystal-clear waters surrounding Korčula and explore its enchanting archipelago aboard a traditional wooden boat or modern yacht. Cruise along the rugged coastline, stopping to swim in secluded bays and snorkel amidst vibrant marine life. Visit nearby islets like Badija and Vrnik, where ancient ruins and pristine beaches await, or embark on a sunset cruise for a romantic evening on the Adriatic.

Shop for local crafts

Explore Korčula's artisanal shops and markets to discover unique handicrafts and souvenirs crafted by local artisans. Browse intricately carved olive wood items, handwoven textiles, and ceramics adorned with traditional motifs, perfect for commemorating your visit to the island. Support local artisans and take home a piece of Korčula's cultural heritage as a cherished keepsake of your time in this enchanting destination.

Stay in boutique accommodations

Enhance your stay in Korčula by choosing boutique accommodations that offer personalized service, stylish accommodations, and authentic experiences. From charming guesthouses tucked away in the heart of Old Town to boutique hotels overlooking the Adriatic Sea, savour the warm hospitality and genuine charm of Korčula's boutique accommodations.

Explore surrounding islands

Venture beyond Korčula to explore the hidden gems of the nearby islands, each offering its own unique attractions and natural beauty. Discover the pristine beaches and lush landscapes of Mljet National Park, the historic charm of Hvar Town, or the secluded coves and crystal-clear waters of Lastovo. Take a day trip or island-hopping excursion to explore the diverse landscapes and cultural heritage of the Dalmatian islands.

Learn basic Croatian phrases

Enhance your cultural experience and connect with the locals by learning a few basic Croatian phrases. While English is widely spoken in tourist areas, making an effort to greet others in Croatian and express gratitude in the local language can enrich your travel experience and foster meaningful interactions with locals.

Respect local customs

Show respect for Korčula's cultural traditions and customs by observing local etiquette and traditions. When visiting religious sites or attending cultural events, dress modestly and behave respectfully to honour the island's heritage and religious practices. By embracing the local way of life with sensitivity and respect, you'll forge deeper connections and create lasting memories of your time in Korčula.

As your time in Korčula draws to a close, take with you cherished memories of ancient architecture, scenic landscapes, and warm hospitality. By following these travel tips and embracing the island's unique charm, you'll embark on a journey that will leave you longing to return to Korčula again and again.

The last sunset: Saying goodbye to Korcula's bliss

Leaving Korčula behind, you carry with you a mosaic of memories that blend the ancient echoes of its past with the vibrant pulse of its present. The island's cultural tapestry, woven with threads of tradition and innovation, has painted a vivid portrait in your mind, inviting you to embrace the beauty and diversity that define Korčula. From the whispers of history in the narrow streets to the tantalizing flavours of local cuisine, each moment spent on this Dalmatian gem has etched a unique chapter in your travel story.

As you bid adieu to Korčula's sun-kissed shores and the welcoming embrace of its inhabitants, you reflect on the harmony of experiences that have enriched your journey. The island's blend of cultural richness, culinary delights, and natural wonders has left an imprint on your soul, beckoning you to revisit its enchanting landscapes and immerse yourself once more in its captivating allure. Korčula's closing sentiments linger like a gentle melody, carrying with them the essence of a place where time seems to stand still, allowing you to savour the magic of this island paradise long after you've set sail for new horizons.

Jay Chandarana

Reflecting on the voyage: Croatia's treasures and tales' farewell

As you reach the end of your journey through Croatia's hidden gems, take a moment to reflect on the myriad experiences that have coloured your adventure. From the sun-kissed shores of the Adriatic to the rugged peaks of the Dinaric Alps, Croatia has unfolded its treasures before you, revealing a tapestry of history, culture, and natural beauty unlike any other.

Throughout your exploration, you've encountered the echoes of ancient civilizations and the whispers of bygone eras, woven into the very fabric of Croatia's landscape. Each incognito destination you've visited has its own story to tell, from the medieval fortresses that stand as sentinels of the past to the quaint villages where time seems to stand still.

You've immersed yourself in the vibrant tapestry of local culture, experiencing first-hand the warmth and hospitality of the Croatian people. Whether sampling traditional delicacies at a family-run konoba or dancing the night away at a lively folk festival, you've been welcomed with open arms into the heart of Croatian life.

But beyond the well-trodden paths lie hidden gems waiting to be discovered by intrepid travellers like yourself. From secret beaches and secluded waterfalls to hidden caves and forgotten ruins, Croatia's treasures are as diverse as they are enchanting, offering endless opportunities for exploration and discovery.

As you bid farewell to the enchanting landscapes and hidden wonders of Croatia explored in this first part of your journey, a new horizon of discovery awaits. Part Two of this eBook promises to peel back the layers of mystery even further, inviting you to delve deeper into the country's rich tapestry of culture and heritage. Prepare to venture off the well-trodden paths and into the lesser-known corners of Croatia, where hidden gems and untold stories lie in wait. From secluded islands and tranquil forests to ancient ruins and traditional villages untouched by time, the next chapter of your adventure promises to be filled with surprises and unforgettable moments.

So, as you eagerly await the next instalment, let your curiosity guide you and your imagination wander. Croatia's secrets are ready to be unveiled, and with each turn of the page, you'll be one step closer to unlocking the mysteries that lie beyond. Get ready to embark on a journey of discovery like no other, as Part Two promises to reveal the hidden treasures that make Croatia truly unique.

Glimpsing Croatia's continued adventure: Previewing what is next

Prepare to embark on a voyage of discovery that will take you deeper into the heart and soul of Croatia. As you bid adieu to the wonders revealed in the first part of this journey, anticipation builds for what lies ahead in Part Two. In the forthcoming chapters, we will delve even further into the hidden corners and untold stories of Croatia. Get ready to explore off-the-beaten-path destinations that promise to captivate your imagination and stir your sense of adventure. From remote islands steeped in folklore to forgotten villages nestled in the embrace of pristine nature, each new revelation will leave you spellbound.

But it is not just the landscapes that will enchant you in Part Two. Prepare to immerse yourself in the vibrant tapestry of Croatian culture, as we uncover age-old traditions and celebrate local festivals that have endured the test of time. From lively folk dances to mouth-watering culinary delights, every encounter will be a feast for the senses, offering a deeper understanding of Croatia's rich heritage.

As the anticipation mounts, so too does the promise of outdoor adventures that await. Whether you are a thrill-seeker craving adrenaline-fueled activities or a nature enthusiast seeking solace in the tranquillity of the wilderness, Part Two has something for everyone. From hiking through rugged mountain ranges to sailing the azure waters of the Adriatic, get ready to answer the call of the wild and embrace the beauty of Croatia's natural landscapes.

But perhaps most thrilling of all is the prospect of uncovering hidden gems that lie just beyond the horizon. Part Two promises to reveal secret treasures that few have had the privilege to witness, inviting you to become a part of Croatia's best-kept secrets. With each discovery, the sense of anticipation grows, fuelling your desire to unearth the mysteries that await.

So, as you eagerly await the next instalment, let your imagination run wild and your anticipation soar. Croatia beckons with promises of adventure, excitement, and discovery, and Part Two is just the beginning of a journey that promises to be nothing short of extraordinary. Get ready to dive in and experience the magic of Croatia in a way you never thought possible.

About the author

JAY CHANDARANA - As an avid explorer and passionate advocate for discovering the lesser-known corners of our world, I am dedicated to embarking on journeys that unravel the mysteries of unexplored destinations. While my travels may not always take me to the most popular tourist spots, my fervor for unearthing hidden gems and sharing them with fellow adventurers is unparalleled.

Despite not having personally visited every place documented in my works, my passion for exploration knows no bounds. Each journey I undertake is meticulously researched, drawing from a wealth of resources, local insights, and firsthand accounts to provide readers with authentic experiences.

My commitment to uncovering the allure of undiscovered locales stems from a desire to transcend conventional travel narratives. Through my writing, I aim to shed light on the richness and diversity of lesser-explored regions, inviting readers to venture beyond the beaten path and immerse themselves in the cultural tapestry of our world.

While renowned destinations certainly hold their allure, I firmly believe that true discovery lies in the exploration of the unfamiliar. It is my mission to inspire others to step off the well-trodden trail and embark on their own adventures, forging connections with places and people they never knew existed.

Join me on a journey of exploration and discovery, as we traverse landscapes both familiar and foreign, uncovering the hidden treasures that await us off the beaten path. Together, let us embark on a quest to broaden our horizons, enrich our perspectives, and ignite a passion for discovery that knows no bounds

Stay connected beyond the pages – join the journey on social media

YouTube: https://www.youtube.com/@incognitodestinations
Instagram: https://www.instagram.com/incognitodestinations
Amazon Catalog: https://amazon.com/author/jaychandarana
Apple books: https://books.apple.com/us/book/revelations-in-the-soul-of-italy/id6479964311?ls=1